The
Street-Smart
Entrepreneur

133 TOUGH LESSONS
I Learned the Hard Way

Jay Goltz

with Jody Oesterreicher

Addicus Books, Inc.
Omaha, Nebraska

An Addicus Nonfiction Book

ISBN 1-886039-33-X

Cover design by George Foster

Cover photo by Barry Elz

Typography by Linda Dageforde

Library of Congress Cataloging-in-Publication Data

Goltz, Jay, 1956-
    The Street-Smart Entrepreneur : 133 tough lessons I learned the hard way / Jay Goltz with Jody Oesterreicher.
      p.   cm.
    Includes index.
    ISBN 1-886039-33-X
    1. Management. 2. Success in business. I. Oesterreicher, Jody, 1961- . II. Title.
HD31.G589 1997   97-33529
658.4'09—DC21   CIP

Addicus Books, Inc.
P.O. Box 45327
Omaha, Nebraska 68145
Web site: http://members.aol.com/addicusbks

Printed in the United States of America
10 9 8 7 6 5 4 3 2 1

Table of Contents

Part II — Being the Boss: There's No Such Thing as Boss School

Part III — Management: If You Want the Job Done Right, Be a Great Manager

Part V — Marketing: What the Hell Is It?

Part VI — Finance: Paper Profits but No Money for Lunch

Part VII — Administration: The Little Things that Can Kill You

To my wife, Sherri, and our three sons—
Mitchell, Aaron, and Jared—
who are constant reminders that business
is a means to an end—not the end.
They make it all worth it.

Acknowledgments

Many people in my life have helped make this book possible. I wish to thank my mother for her many years of nurturing and my father for being a role model—a man who was hard working, has an unshakable sense of responsibility, and did everything he could for the customers of his dime store. I am grateful as well to my sister Sharon and her husband, Alan Rosen, for their continuing support. Alan was the only person who told me to "go for it" when I was considering starting my business.

I especially wish to thank all my employees, past and present, who have shared both losses and successes with me through this journey. I would like to acknowledge Jody Oesterreicher for her invaluable assistance in writing this book. Also, my thanks goes to Bob Sapio, a fellow entrepreneur, for his suggestions on the early drafts of this book.

I am grateful to Dr. Joe Mancuso of the CEO Club and Dr. Jan Zupnick of the Entrepreneurship Forum, who gave me the first opportunity to interact with other business owners and introduced me to public speaking.

Finally, I express my warmest thanks to my customers who have supported me, guided me, taught me, and helped me grow along the way.

Introduction

Those of us who grew up in the 1970s, were expected to go to college, obtain advanced degrees, and become doctors, lawyers, or accountants. Something of a conformist, I went to college and pursued a bachelor's degree in accounting. By my senior year, however, I was having serious reservations about becoming an accountant. I made an appointment with the career counselor. I told her I had hated both grade school and high school and wasn't much more enthusiastic about college. All she said was, "If you really want to get somewhere today, you need a graduate degree. I suggest you pursue a master's in accounting."

She heard not a single word I had said. That was my first hint there would be little support from the academic community for entrepreneurship. By then I was fairly sure the answer to my uncertainty didn't lie in academia. It was difficult for me to imagine sitting through another advanced accounting course or studying for the CPA exam. I was more inclined to jump off a cliff than pursue a graduate degree. I didn't know what I was going to do because I didn't think I had any special talents. My educational background wasn't terribly impressive, either. It wasn't the best time in my life.

I'd worked for the picture framing business of my friend Bruce Teitelbaum's father while I was in high school. In college Bruce and I sold frames to artists on our own. I enjoyed picture framing, so after I graduated I thought I'd try to make a career out of it. My other friends said, "Are you crazy? You're going to waste your degree?" By then I was more concerned about wasting my life doing something I didn't really want to do than wasting my degree. I founded my business with next to nothing in 1978, setting up shop in a low-rent, run-down, former manufacturing district on Chicago's North Side. I came up with the name Artists' Frame Service because I initially catered to artists.

While I was toiling alone in my little frame shop, my contemporaries were being mentored by the senior people at their firms. The junior accountants, lawyers, and copywriters were learning the ropes from their partners and creative directors. The medical students were being trained by their resident and attending physicians. Some of my friends went into family businesses and were groomed by their fathers.

I soon realized that when you go into business for yourself, you're not mentored by anyone—you're tortured by everybody. The torture begins the day you hang your shingle. It doesn't take long before you start making mistakes, but it can take years before you *realize* you have made them and another few years before you're able to straighten them out.

I use the word "torture" because making mistakes in business can be painful, and I mean excruciatingly painful. It's torture when you make one bad hire after another because you don't know how to interview prospective employees. It's torture when you finally scrape together enough money to launch a mini-ad campaign and it flops because the advertising agency didn't understand your business. It's torture when you discover one day that you can't pay your bills because your business has been growing so fast that you have neglected your accounting. The torture doesn't stop after you've been in business for a few years, either. Every time you take your business to a new level, there are new mistakes just waiting to be made.

Today, I make few major mistakes. That's only because during my first fifteen years in business I made every single mistake in the book. When I say "in the book," I mean it figuratively because I never could find any books that spell out the pitfalls of running your own business.

Despite an endless string of errors, I managed to grow Artists' Frame Service from $70,000 in sales in 1978 to $10 million in sales in 1997. Artists' Frame Service is considered a phenomenon in the framing industry. It's the world's largest retail, custom picture-framing facility in an industry that's comprised largely of ma-and-pa shops; these shops usually average annual sales of about $200,000. Even mid-size shops lag far behind Artists' Frame Service in volume.

Fortunately, while I was making all of those mistakes, I also was doing a few things right. I used to be in awe of framers who operated successful businesses. I thought they knew everything there was to know about picture framing. I wondered if I ever would reach their level. Even before I opened my own place, however, I began to question whether these guys really were so smart. It started when I realized there is no reason to make customers wait three to eight weeks for a framing job. I introduced one-week service, and customers loved it. Suddenly I saw there was money to be made by better execution of an old concept. Artists' Frame Service didn't reinvent the picture frame, we reinvented the framing business. I began to introduce other innovations including pickup, delivery and installation, and the availability of an unparalleled selection of in-stock mouldings. I hired sales people with art and design backgrounds and trained them thoroughly. I put systems in place to help ensure my customers weren't just satisfied but thrilled with our work.

The customer service thing came naturally to me, but it was years before I realized I had any special talents in that department. I learned most everything I know about customer service from working at my father's dime store as a kid. Institutionalizing customer service at a company with more than a hundred employees, however, is another story. Like management, marketing, and finance, I had to learn that aspect of the business from scratch.

Today my business encompasses retail, manufacturing, and service, giving me a broad business perspective few people enjoy. I wrote this book because I want to help other people in business avoid at least some of the pain I experienced. I believe you can learn from other people's mistakes. I give presentations on entrepreneurship and customer service at trade shows, conferences, and forums across the country. Most of the people in the audience are struggling with the same issues I've struggled with over the years. They're thirsting for information from someone who has been there.

That's what this book is about. It tells you what you need to know to survive in business. There are no academic theories in this book, no superficial feel-good messages, just the blood-and-guts reality of running a business every day.

Jay Goltz
Chicago, Illinois

Part I – Start Ups:

Starting Up without Throwing Up

If You Don't Want to Answer to Anyone, Find a Nice Cave

What I Used to Think: When you go into business for yourself, you don't have to answer to anyone.

Nobody Told Me: When you go into business for yourself, you have to answer to *everybody*. You have to answer to your customers, your employees, your landlord, your neighbors, the IRS — everybody. You may not have to take orders and you may have more control of your destiny, but you're accountable to everybody. There's a long list of reasons why people go into business for themselves. They're great salespersons, they're natural leaders, they're ambitious, they have highly marketable skills, or they have a vision. Going into business for yourself so you don't have to answer to anyone is the reason least likely to result in success.

Lesson #1: Going into business for yourself is more responsibility than you can possibly imagine.

Great Ideas Can Be Hazardous to Your Health

What I Used to Think: You think it's a great idea, your wife and kids think it's a great idea, and your friends think it's a great idea. It *must* be a great idea.

Nobody Told Me: You could come up with the most hare-brained idea and find a dozen friends who would say it's great. Why? Because they don't know any better. Because they don't want to burst your bubble. Because they admire your ambition. When you have an idea, discuss it with some-one who has enough business smarts and objectivity to say with authority, "I don't think that idea will work. Here's why." Or, "It's a great idea. Let me tell you why."

Several years ago I stumbled into the opening celebration of an ice cream parlor near my home in suburban Chicago. A corporate executive had opened the shop. He had planned for his wife to run the place until his retirement, when they would run it together. That night there was a big crowd of well-wishers. Everybody was smiling. The future looked bright. I went in there on a Saturday about a month later, and it was very quiet. The wife, husband, and their eldest child were working behind the counter. They looked disappointed but hopeful. I came back a month after that and found the wife working alone. The place was empty. I returned a few months later and found the windows covered with newspa-pers. The shop had closed.

I don't know enough about the ice cream business or about the personality of this corporate executive to say why the business failed. But I do know summers are short in

Chicago, and running a small business is a far cry from running a corporation. I suspect this guy's friends and family told him the ice cream parlor was a great idea. But I doubt he thought it through very carefully either from a business or personal perspective.

It's crucial to conduct a careful business analysis and make a business plan before starting or purchasing a business. It also is important to talk to lots of people, like the owners of similar businesses, potential customers, a lawyer, an accountant, and anyone else who can shed some light on what you might be getting yourself into.

Lesson #2: Behind every failed business are a dozen friends who said it was a great idea.

Have You Thought about Your Assets Lately?

What I Used to Think: Hard work is the surest route to success.

Nobody Told Me: If hard work is the key to success, most people would be successful. Leveraging your assets probably is as crucial to success as hard work. When I say "assets" I don't just mean what you own. I mean anything you can use to your advantage. The kid who goes into business with his father may be leveraging his parentage. The guy who makes it big in sales may be leveraging his personality. The woman who opens a visiting nurse's service may be leveraging her experience as a nurse and administrator. You can leverage anything, including who you know, where you're located, and what ideas you have.

To get my business off the ground, I leveraged three assets: my best friend's father had a picture-framing business, I was well versed in customer service from having worked at my father's dime store, and I had a good head for math. The key to leveraging your assets is to take inventory of what you have. Some people do start from scratch, but they usually take longer to succeed than those people who use everything they have to fuel their ambitions.

Lesson #3: If you've got it, use it, even if it's just a great smile.

Putting the Competition under the Microscope

What I Used to Think: The best competition is no competition.

Nobody Told Me: Competition is one of the primary indicators of demand. If there's no competition, there may not be a market for your product or service. If you're trying to break into a competitive market, however, first do a competition analysis.

Location may be a vital factor in your success, whether you're a retailer, wholesaler, or manufacturer. Governmental agencies, universities, think tanks, and even the company that produces the Yellow Pages publish information that may help you determine the best location for your business.

If you want to give your competitors a run for their money, you have to know their weaknesses. Consider posing as a customer to find out more about the competition—how they do business and who their customers are. Your business will have a better chance of succeeding in a competitive market if you provide better prices, quality, or service than your competitors. If the market is saturated, there's nothing you can do to improve on the existing businesses, or they have unassailable competitive advantages, you might be better off getting into something else.

Lesson #4: It's easier to steal a share of the market than to create a market.

The Money Pit

What I Used to Think: Your start-up costs are pretty straight-forward.

Nobody Told Me: A little thing called *negative cash flow*, can blow the lid off your business before you ever have a chance to make a go of it. One of the keys to a successful start-up is to begin with enough capital to keep your business afloat until it breaks even. One of the biggest mistakes people make with their start-ups is underestimating the time it takes for their businesses to be up and running. You have to hire employees, train them, and often replace them because they don't work out. The time between starting and running the business can be weeks or months. Guess what, your new employees have to be paid during this phase!

That's why you have to project what your break-even point and how much working capital your business needs until that time. You're going to lose money until then, and it's difficult to raise fresh capital when you're in a hole. It's smarter to raise the capital on the front end, leaving yourself with a substantial cushion so that you don't run out in the middle of the game. There are few things more heart-wrenching in business than blowing a successful start-up just because you ran out of cash. It's like digging an oil well and running out of money for drilling when you're two feet away from hitting oil.

Lesson #5: Starting a business is a money pit. Be prepared by having plenty of working capital up front.

Don't Turn Up Your Nose at "Stale" Old Concepts

What I Used to Think: You have to come up with a new concept to be a business success.

Nobody Told Me: If you want to be successful in business, execute well. If you want to get rich quickly come up with a new concept. Most businesses aren't born from new concepts, yet they make money year after year. Ideally, you should come up with a new concept *and* execute it well.

More often than not, however, I have seen hot new businesses that lose steam after a few years because they fall short in the area of execution. A business may come up with a new concept, have great marketing, capture the imagination of the public, and generate excitement about their product or service. They initially have little or no competition, so their margins are strong. Those factors enable the owners to rapidly expand their business. When other players step into the market, however, they have to shift gears. They no longer can coast on great publicity and have to focus on execution.

Execution has been the key to the success of my business from day one. I started my company realizing there was money to be made by better executing an old concept. My company didn't reinvent the picture frame, we reinvented the framing business. We raised the level of customer service far beyond the industry standard and implemented systems to ensure that our customers not only received outstanding service but also excellent quality. I always am looking for that hot new concept, but execution has served me well over the years and will continue to be a factor in any new business ventures I undertake.

Lesson #6: New concepts are powerful, but execution ultimately determines how successful you are.

Price, Quality, Service ---- Pick Two

What I Used to Think: You have to give your customers the best prices, outstanding quality, and exceptional service.

Nobody Told Me: No company can give the best prices, outstanding quality, *and* exceptional service and survive in business very long. Most successful companies usually give two out of three of those things in one combination or another.

Discount stores, for instance, provide low prices and good-quality merchandise. But the service is nothing to write home about. You just don't find many well-informed or experienced salespeople at discount stores, despite what their multimillion-dollar advertising campaigns tell you. Discount store employees often are low-paid, part-time workers. Some discount stores are better than others, but their service rarely compares to the service you will find at a boutique or even a better department store. Federal Express, on the other hand, is an example of a company that provides excellent service and outstanding quality but not the lowest prices.

I'm hard pressed to name a single company that provides the lowest prices, highest quality, *and* best service. The key to business success is to provide two of the three. I always wanted to provide a high-quality product and exceptional service, but I also wanted my prices to be the lowest in town. I soon realized it costs money to provide service and quality, so I had to adjust my prices. I am not the cheapest framer in town, but my prices are competitive and, by far, I offer the best value. I am able to do this because I buy materials directly from manufacturers at a considerable savings.

A lot of framing companies with low prices have gone out of business because their service stunk or their quality was poor. The market has to support whatever combination of price, quality, and service you are willing to provide. There are discount food chains that thrive and discount drug stores that fail. Why? Because success for them depends on whether their low prices generate enough business to make up for their smaller margins.

That's why when you start your own business, you need to analyze the market, your personality, your assets, and a dozen other factors before deciding what combination of price, quality, and service you want to provide.

Lesson #7: Two out of three ain't bad when you're talking about price, quality, and service.

Get to Know Your Local Pawnboker

What I Used to Think: If you have nothing, you have nothing to lose by going into business for yourself.

Nobody Told Me: Unless you're independently wealthy, have wealthy parents, or have an investor, it's difficult to make it through the start-up without putting everything you own on the line. I've never heard of banks making loans without collateral. I'm surprised by how many people think banks will hand money over to you for nothing but your signature and X amount of interest.

At a speaking engagement, I told the audience, "Banks don't care about your hopes and dreams. They want collateral." A person in the audience raised his hand and said, "You're wrong. I just went to my bank and borrowed $25,000." I said, "Really? Do you own a house?" He said, "Yes." "Did you sign for the loan personally?" I asked. "Yes," he answered. "Well then," I said, "they're using your house as collateral." He looked stunned.

Another time, someone I met at a business conference told me that he borrowed money to buy a multimillion-dollar business, even though he had limited assets. I wondered if he knew something I didn't, until we met again a few weeks later. He casually mentioned that his wealthy father co-signed his loan.

Like a lot of business owners, I had no one to loan money to me, provide equity, or even co-sign my loans. I was reluctant to take on an investor or partner. I had nothing but a small amount of savings and had to put up everything I owned as collateral for loans. If your business fails, you could lose your home. If your business succeeds, it's not like you just pay back the loan and that's the end of it. If you want to continue growing your business, you probably will have to take out additional loans. It's not uncommon for business owners to take on tremendous bank debt and, in some instances, to borrow all the way to the wall.

Lesson #8: If you want to start and grow your business without investors (including Dad), be prepared to hock everything, including your class ring.

Your Grocery Bagger Might Be a Better Person to Go into Business with Than Your Best Friend

What I Used to Think: There's no better person to go into business with than someone you know, like, and trust.

Nobody Told Me: I didn't give it much thought when I went into the framing business with a friend. I just knew that his father was doing OK in framing, that my friend and I got along well, and that I didn't know what else to do with my life. My friend dropped out of the business shortly after we started, so I don't know whether the partnership would have worked in the long term. I've observed a lot of partnerships over the years, however, and found there are some common denominators among both those that succeed and those that fail.

Most people go into business together because they've been friends since kindergarten, or, you know, "I like to cook and you like people, so we'll open a restaurant. I'll be the chef, and you'll be the maitre d'." These partnerships are frequently doomed because the people involved fail to consider whether their talents and abilities are complimentary or whether they possess the necessary skills to run a particular kind of business. Sometimes one partner brings more to the table than the other partner. As the business becomes more successful, the more valuable partner may realize he/she is the one who makes it work and may begin to resent it. The less valuable partner seldom agrees that he/she is not pulling enough weight. It can get very ugly.

Partnerships that begin as strategic alliances, on the other hand, have a better chance of surviving. The partners get together because their combined talents and abilities are likely to ensure the success of their business. Corporations merge to create healthier companies, but when it comes to the small business sector, you find people forming partnerships because they're best buddies. Sometimes you even see three or four friends starting companies, and that really is a joke. By the end of the first year or so, it's a safe bet the partnership will be down to two people.

There are some people who say, "Never have a partner. It's the worst thing in the world." I disagree. Many partnerships fail miserably, but there are wonderful partnerships that result in successful businesses because the partners have formed strategic alliances.

Lesson #9: Going into business with friends just because they're your friends is like betting on a horse just because you like its name.

The Unimaginable Life of an Entrepreneur

What I Used to Think: Your life as an entrepreneur is no different than other people's lives, except that you work for yourself not for someone else.

Nobody Told Me: Starting a business is like pushing a boulder up a hill. The second you stop pushing, it will roll down on top of you. If you start a business from scratch, there's no momentum. You could even say there's *negative* momentum. Your revenues lag far behind your expenses, and you just have to push, and push, and push some more to get additional business. I saw a newspaper advertisement recently for a franchise. It showed a guy sitting at a desk littered with paper. The copy read something like, "Are you fed up?" It painted self-employment as an antidote to job stress. I had to laugh because I assumed the guy was a new business owner.

It takes a long time before you get some positive momentum in the form of repeat customers and referrals. For years I put in seventy hours a week. I remember coming home late one evening and seeing my neighbor walk by with a softball bat. He'd been playing softball in the park since five o'clock. That's when I realized my life was very different than the lives of my contemporaries. A short time later, I got married and started a family. While my friends were starting to invest their money in pension funds, I was feeding nearly every penny I earned back into the business.

That's a thumbnail sketch of my life and those of many other business owners I know. It does get better, but not overnight. Today I put in fewer hours, have fewer worries, and have manageable debt.

Lesson #10: Starting a business is one of the most difficult challenges a person can undertake *and* one of the most rewarding...if it succeeds.

Crystal Gazing for Real

What I Used to Think: You don't need a vision for your business. It's not as if you're trying to shape an entire industry.

Nobody Told Me: There's a lot of money in being a visionary no matter what you do. It probably is less crucial for me to be a visionary than it is for someone in the computer industry, for example. But having a vision sure helps. The two major components of vision are the ability to foresee consumer and industry trends and the ability to define just where you want your company to go.

In the early 1980s, I noticed that in my business the artworks our customers were framing were getting larger while their cars were getting smaller. It often took two persons to carry a framed picture to a customer's car. Getting the picture in the car was another production. I instituted delivery service in response to these trends, and it was a tremendous success. It also fit in with the business trend of providing superior customer service.

More recently I developed the vision of making my company an institution. That vision now guides many of my business decisions. It pushed me to begin thinking about what I'd have to do to make my company an institution. I realized that if I wanted people to think of Artists' Frame Service as the place to go for framing, I'd have to create a beautiful, state-of-the-art showroom. I installed, among other things, a computer system that calculates how much material we need for each framing job, and special lighting, so what customers see in our showroom is the same as what they would see at home. Now, whenever I have doubts about spending money on some improvement, I ask myself whether it'll help me achieve my vision.

Vision also involves staying on top of trends in other industries that may affect your business. If your bank undergoes a merger, for instance, think about what that means for your company.

Lesson #11: Whether or not you see change coming, it will have an impact on you.

There's More to Success Than Money

What I Used to Think: If you keep your nose to the grindstone and make sacrifices for your business, you'll be successful and happy.

Nobody Told Me: There are a lot of unhappy millionaires. People who put all of their energy into work frequently wind up with unhappy children, unhappy spouses, and unhappy lives. Bookshelves are filled with autobiographies written by successful business people. But if their spouses and children wrote about them, I'm sure they would tell a different story.

If you have a happy family and want to keep it, you have to make some compromises with your business. When you devote all of your energy to work, your family pays a price, and you eventually do, too. Many people lose their families because they fail to find a balance between work and home. If you fail to find a balance between work and family, you may become a divorce statistic.

I'm not suggesting that you attend every one of your kid's Little League baseball games. That kind of inflexibility could cause serious problems at work. You might try instead showing up for half of those games. Instead of trying to grow your business 30 percent annually, consider aiming for a growth rate of 15 percent. Maybe it's OK if you miss a few business functions and make fewer contacts. It may cost you some business, but the payoff for your family life may be worth it.

That said, there may be times when your company is growing and it's necessary to spend additional time away from your family. Whatever the case, it never hurts to ask yourself from time to time whether it really is necessary to do something that keeps you away from home.

Lesson #12: Wealth is just one barometer of success.

A Healthy Business Starts with a Healthy Body

What I Used to Think: When you're young and strong, you don't have to think about your health.

Nobody Told Me: Health is your best long-term investment. When I started my business fresh out of college, like many young people I took my health for granted. My body soon sent a message to me, however, that I had better pay attention. I had been suffering from severe intestinal pain for many months before going to an internist, who gave me a prescription that failed to provide relief.

I read a magazine article shortly thereafter that clued me into the real problem. The article described the link between intestinal pain and stress. I made some changes at work to reduce the amount of stress I was experiencing. I also began exercising regularly and eating better so I would have more energy to handle those stressful situations you just can't avoid.

It's easy to take your health for granted when you're young, but it's difficult to develop healthy habits when you're older. Neglecting your health in the long run is a detriment to your business. Health problems may distract you from business, if not prevent you from being able to work altogether. The time you invest in your health, no matter what your age, will pay high dividends. You will experience the payoff in your energy level, mental acuity, emotional well-being, and ability to deal effectively with stress.

If you have stress-related health problems or deteriorating health, it's time for you to re-evaluate where you're going and how you're getting there. Make your health a top priority because all the success in the world means nothing if you're unhealthy.

Lesson #13: Taking care of your health is one job you can't delegate.

Part II – Being the Boss:

There's No Such Thing as Boss School

If You Were Unpopular in High School, You're One Step Ahead of the Game

What I Used to Think: As the boss, if you're nice to people and treat them fairly, they'll like and respect you.

Nobody Told Me: Ha-ha-ha-ha-ha! If you're in a position of authority, no matter how nice and fair you are, some people will dislike you. You have to accept that. There are many times when, for the good of your business, you will have to say or do things that upset people. It's naive to think if you fire someone who has been doing a bad job, he/she will say, "Oh, listen, I totally understand. If I were in your shoes, I'd do the same thing."

I've got a dozens of examples, but I'll only mention a case in point. I sent an employee who had been with my company for a few months to a computer training class. She quit the day after the class. I couldn't resist asking her, "Don't you feel a bit guilty that I just paid for you to take that class?" She, of course, said, "No." There wasn't a damn thing I could do about it. There often isn't when someone treats you unfairly.

Your unpopularity doesn't stop with your employees. If you have to cut off a customer who has unpaid receivables, he/she may tell everyone what a jerk you are. It goes with the territory, so you have to develop a thick skin. My goal is for my employees, customers, and vendors to respect me and enjoy working with my company. But I accept that some of them may not.

Lesson #14: Being the boss isn't a popularity contest.

31

Values Don't Break, They Crumble

What I Used to Think: If you hire good employees, they'll do great work.

Nobody Told Me: Every great quarterback has a great coach. The boss at a great company has to be *demanding, uncompromising,* and *intolerant* in setting company standards and in working with employees to maintain those standards. I've never heard of a crummy company with a crummy boss that succeeded in business because an employee has said, "Gee, Mr. Boss, let's improve our service and the quality of our product." Behind every great company is someone who has said, "We're going to make an excellent product and provide great service."

Setting high standards means you're *demanding.* Maintaining those standards means you're *uncompromising.* Values don't break, they crumble. Say you're in the trucking business. You decide to provide 48-hour service. That's your standard. Your employees get behind it, but after the first big snowstorm you're unable to make good on your promise of 48-hour deliveries because all the roads are closed. A few weeks later there's another bad snowstorm, but the roads are open. You decide no 48-hour deliveries because it's snowing *almost* as bad as the time when the roads were closed. A few weeks later it's pouring rain, so you waive the 48-hour rule again. Another month down the road and you decide a particular customer can live without 48-hour delivery. Then it's *all* of your small customers and on, and on, and on, until you no longer provide 48-hour service to anyone.

That kind of disintegration happens with everything. An employee gets something in his/her eye, and for the next week everyone wears safety glasses. A week later, a few employees have stopped wearing them. A few weeks after that, half of the employees are wearing safety glasses. A month later, nobody is wearing them. A month after that, they have no idea where their safety glasses are. There's no standard or policy that won't be compromised if you don't monitor it constantly and aren't uncompromising in your insistence that it be upheld.

Being *intolerant,* the boss's third major responsibility, means you get rid of employees who continually challenge your company's standards — period.

Lesson #15: A company is only as good as the boss.

The In-Your-Face World of Business

What I Used to Think: Nice people avoid confrontations.

Nobody Told Me: You can't manage without confrontation. The meek might inherit the earth, but they'll go broke in business. Not everyone has the same standards of behavior as you do. There are times when business owners have to confront employees, customers, and vendors either because they're acting irresponsibly or making unreasonable demands. Some people mistake kindness for weakness and try to take advantage of you. You have to stand up to those people. Your business depends on it.

Having to fire an employee probably is one of the most difficult situations business owners confront. I know many employers who keep unproductive workers on the payroll for years rather than fire them. Their businesses suffer and in some instances fail.

Whether it's giving unwarranted discounts, extending credit beyond terms, or taking back merchandise, there comes a time when you have to say no to a customer.

Suppose a longtime vendor's quality and service decline. You have to confront the vendor and let him/her know that you no longer will accept substandard materials or service. Years ago, a well-known business forms manufacturer sent me invoices with sloppy borders, unclear printing, and several other obvious flaws. I called the manager to complain. His response remains etched in my memory. He said, and I quote, "As a standard in the industry, these are good forms." If I were meek, I would have let it go at that. But these forms were terrible! Even though I was still somewhat naive, I just had to say something. I told the guy, "You have pathetic standards. The forms will be waiting for you on my dock." He immediately changed his tune and asked how his company could make it up to me. I agreed to a huge discount on the forms and a promise that the next order would be printed perfectly.

Lesson #16: Being the boss isn't for the faint of heart.

Getting to Know Your Own Strength

What I Used to Think: Employees treat you the same way other people do.

Nobody Told Me: Bosses wield the power and authority of a mother. Employees watch everything the boss says and does. If you have a bad day and walk around the office fuming, employees may assume you're angry with them about that order last week or something else they did. Some of them may conclude business is bad and begin worrying they'll be laid off. I've learned to keep my emotions in check to avoid needlessly upsetting employees. Conversely, it's important to recognize that you can make an employee's day just by saying, "Hey, Sue, you're always there when I need you."

As sensitive as you are to your employees, however, don't expect much sensitivity from them. A few years ago, I had to make a tough business decision. I said to my controller, "You know, it's funny, no one ever gives moral support to the boss. No one ever says, 'Hey, I know it was difficult to fire old Joe, but I give you credit for always doing what's best for the company' or 'Hey, I know we lost that order, but we'll dig in next week and get more business.'" Well, my controller just looked at me and said, "Oh, that's easy. Everyone knows the boss isn't human." The sad part is she was only half joking. There are times when you could fire Charles Manson, and even though everyone knows he is a psychopath, they still would say, "Oh, did you hear? He fired good old Chuck."

Lesson #17: You're the big bad boss, no matter how nice you are. Get used to it.

The Vein-Popping Zone

What I Used to Think: You have to be emotional to succeed in business.

Nobody Told Me: Emotions can be a powerful tool for motivating employees, selling your product, and driving yourself and your business forward. They also can be incredibly destructive. There are times when you must draw on your emotions and times when you must rely on careful analysis to accomplish your goals. Anger, of course, can be a highly destructive emotion in its rawest form. Going off on an employee who made a mistake, for instance, only makes matters worse. The employee feels terrible, and the morale of other employees suffers.

When someone makes a mistake, it's more important to figure out how to fix it and prevent similar mistakes than it is to vent your anger. If you get upset over every mistake, you eventually will become a basket case. You have to learn how to control not only the expression of your anger but also the anger itself. It also may be appropriate to make some changes in the workplace. If an employee is making too many mistakes or having an inordinate number of accidents, for example, the answer may be to fire him/her. It's arguably kinder to do that than scream at someone who, for whatever reason, can't make the grade.

Letting your emotions guide your business decisions also presents problems. Maybe you're bidding on a huge order. You know how much you have to charge to make money on it. You hate the thought of your competitor beating you out, however, so you come in with a low bid. You get the job and now have the honor of losing money on it.

Maybe you realize that your profit margins are way too low, so you decide to raise prices 5 percent to strengthen your business. Then a good customer comes in and lays into you for fifteen minutes about how your company no longer is such a great deal. You're overcome by the fear of losing customers and decide to hold off on price increases. If you thought the matter through, however, you'd see that you might lose this customer, but you won't lose all or even most of your customers. Moreover, the higher profit margins you realize on the customers who stay with you will more than make up for any business you lose.

Lesson #18: Emotions can be a leadership asset and a management liability.

Joined at the Hip

What I Used to Think: If a long-term relationship goes bad, you just get out of it.

Nobody Told Me: Business owners must be careful about entering into long-term relationships with customers, employees, or vendors. When someone offers you business, or you just have interviewed the ideal prospective employee, it's easy to get caught up in the excitement of the moment and make all sorts of promises you may be unable to keep. I never promise promotions or raises, for example, to new employees. I let them know if everything goes well they may wind up in a higher-paying position, but if a new venture fails or I run into some other problem, they may lose their job.

As far as customers go, I never provide discounts without contingencies. I offer, for instance, to frame their posters for a certain price so long as they order a specific number of frames. I also let them know I may have to raise my prices after a fixed period of time to cover cost increases. Similarly, I make no open-ended agreements with vendors. I only commit to purchasing their goods so long as they remain the most competitive suppliers and maintain their quality standards. It's a good idea with any special deal to review the terms after a specified amount of time.

Lesson #19: Long-term relationships are easy to get into and hard to get out of. Choose your partners carefully and always have an escape clause.

Of Lawsuits and Land Mines

What I Used to Think: You don't have to worry about lawsuits if you have a good lawyer.

Nobody Told Me: Every boss has to be a part-time lawyer. If you're unfamiliar with the law, how will you ever know when you should consult with your lawyer? We live in a highly litigious society and must do everything we can to avoid lawsuits. There's been an explosion of employee lawsuits in the last decade, partially fueled by an overabundance of lawyers, many of whom file frivolous lawsuits on a contingency basis.

Resolve to look for new hires before you need them desperately so that you can interview more prospects and screen them more thoroughly. Educate yourself on hiring techniques and management practices to help avoid employee lawsuits.

You also should research your vendors. Business owners often rely on legal contracts to avoid lawsuits with vendors, but by the time you have to rely on a contract, it's too late. You've spent thousands of dollars on legal fees and are spending more time with your lawyers than with your customers. Contracts can help protect you, but they won't save you. I'd rather have a weak contract with a reputable company than a great contract with an unreliable company. Just as it's foolish to drive down a treacherous road thinking, "It's OK. I've got my seat belt on," it's foolish to get involved with a company you know nothing about thinking, "It's OK I've got a good legal contract."

Customer lawsuits may be the easiest ones to avoid. The rule is to never make promises you can't or may not be able to keep. Act responsibly when there's a problem with a customer, and chances are you not only will avert a lawsuit but also hold onto the customer.

Lesson #20: You might have the world's most profitable business, but one nasty lawsuit could wipe out all of your profits, a lot of your time, and a good portion of your brain.

The Motivation Myth

What I Used to Think: Motivation is the key to success.

Nobody Told Me: Motivation is one of the most misunderstood business concepts. I used to go to motivational seminars, watch motivational tapes, read motivational books, and then come into the office psyched up to take over the world. I soon became frustrated, however, because I was unable to achieve the results the motivational experts promised. I was motivated, but that wasn't enough. Ironically, the more I tried to practice what the motivational experts preached, the more frustrated and unmotivated I became.

I eventually realized being motivated is only half the battle. You also have to know what you're doing. You may be motivated to pursue a career as a professional golfer and practice on the golf course every day, but never make a cent because you lack natural talent and proper instruction. The same is true in business, and I'm not talking about going to school for an MBA. I'm talking about figuring out what you're doing wrong and fixing it and learning how to do things right from other people in business. You also have to provide your employees with information and training. The most motivated employees become unmotivated if they're unable to do their jobs properly.

Lesson #21: Motivation without education leads to frustration.

The Road to Hell is Paved with Yes-Men

What I Used to Think: People tell you when they think you're wrong.

Nobody Told Me: People stand around and watch you dig your own grave. If you lose your cool and scream at an employee, no one at your company is going to say, "Hey, that was really destructive. You need to try to control your temper." I want people to question my judgment, monitor my behavior, and disagree with my conclusions. The last thing I need is someone who's going to support me in my mistakes. I've been in meetings where nearly everyone agrees on something, and then one brave soul says, "I think that's a bad idea. Here's why." As it turns out, that person is right.

The naturally hierarchical structure of most companies breeds yes-men. But employers can make the situation much worse by demeaning or ignoring employees who disagree with them or by rewarding employees who go along with them. I've heard an employer ask an employee for an opinion and then say, "That's the worst idea I've ever heard." I try to create an environment where employees feel comfortable expressing their opinions. I also try to hire people, especially for upper management positions, who are naturally inclined to speak their minds. If someone always agrees with you, then you have a problem.

Lesson #22: Yes-men are made, not born. There's nothing more dangerous in business than yes-men.

The Fine Art of Delegating Authority

What I Used to Think: You tell people what to do, and they do it.

Nobody Told Me: If you have a gun to their heads, maybe. I've never had much trouble delegating authority, but it took me a while to learn how to do it well. You have to make your expectations clear and follow up to make sure your employees are doing what you asked them to do. You also have to expect screwups when you delegate authority. I avoid delegating jobs that will cost me a bundle if someone makes a mistake.

After a few years in business, I was eager to follow the advice about delegating authority that I'd read in so many management books. In Chicago you used to have to put a new vehicle sticker on your windshield right before the New Year. I said to myself, "You know, I should delegate this vehicle sticker thing. The boss shouldn't spend his time scraping off and replacing vehicle stickers in the freezing cold." So, admittedly, starting small, I delegated the job to one of my production people and felt pretty good when he told me he had taken care of it without any trouble. When I went out to the car that night, I saw that the sticker was halfway up the window instead of in the lower corner. I drove around with that sticker obstructing my view for a year. It was a painful reminder of my failure to delegate authority well.

The following year, I said to myself, "You really didn't understand delegation last year. When you delegate you have to give thorough instructions." So I gave my employee a razor blade, a paper towel for the scrapings, and instructions to place the new sticker one inch from the bottom and one inch from the side of the windshield. I had a car and a van, so I told him to take care of the car after he finished with the van. He came into my office a little while later. I said, "Did you finish the job?" He said, "Kinda." So I said, "What do you mean, kinda?" "Well, I had a little problem," he said. "I can't find the razor blade." So there was a razor blade floating around somewhere in the car that I drove with my family. I began to wonder whether delegation was such a good idea after all.

The next year, however, I refused to give up. I asked another employee to do the job. I gave him detailed instructions and just one sticker at a time so he'd have to put them on the right vehicles. I also told him to keep an eye on the razor blade. He came back to my office ten minutes later and handed the vehicle sticker to me in one sheet. I never have been able to scrape a sticker off in one piece like that. I thought to myself, "I've become some kind of delegation guru. I got the right guy, gave him the right tools and clear instructions, and he did a better job than I could have." I gave him the other sticker. He was gone for ten minutes, then twenty. Finally, thirty minutes later, he walked into my office as white as a sheet. I said, "Did you take care of it?" He said, "No, I broke the windshield." As it turned out he had used a blowtorch in subzero temperatures to remove the stickers.

There are two lessons here. First if you see an employee walking around with a blowtorch, ask where he/she is going. The more important lesson, which took me weeks to accept, is that screwups happen. It's easy to forget that the thirty other jobs you delegated that week went smoothly when you're in the midst of a crisis. The windshield cost a couple hundred dollars. But if I had done everything myself, (as the old saying goes, if you want it done right, you have to do it yourself) it would have cost me much more. I would have spent all of my time doing maintenance, deliveries, writing ad copy, and everything else instead of running my business.

Lesson #23: Screwups happen when you delegate authority. Deal with them. Don't stop delegating.

A Perfect Nutcase

What I Used to Think: Demand nothing less than perfection from yourself and your employees.

Nobody Told Me: Perfectionism can be an illness. It's admirable to pursue perfection but impractical to expect perfection. Perfection is more or less attainable depending on what product or service you provide. If you're talking about a courier service, it may be possible to achieve perfection simply by picking up or delivering a package by 10:30 A.M. If you're talking about a snowplowing service, it never will be possible to achieve perfection by removing every speck of snow from someone's driveway or parking lot. It may, however, be possible to achieve perfection by plowing after every snowstorm.

It's nearly impossible to achieve perfection in the framing business. We do most of our work by hand and use wood mouldings, cotton fiber mat boards, and other materials that have natural variations. I came up with a standard of excellence whereby it's OK for a framing job to go out the door if it looks perfect...at arm's length. If you take time to examine at a speck from three inches away, it is counterproductive. We could never get a job finished.

The law of diminishing returns applies to quality control. If I were any more exacting with framing than I am now, few customers would notice. Few customers, however, would fail to notice the price increases I would have to implement to make those improvements.

I also have learned that there's a difference between being demanding and being a perfectionist. I think perfectionism is a sickness that can be demoralizing for both you and your employees. If employees do an excellent job more than 99 percent of the time, how can it be helpful to reproach them on those few occasions when they fall just a little short? You'll make yourself sick if you expect perfection either from yourself or your employees.

Lesson #24: The goal of perfection contributes to a well-run business. The expectation of perfection contributes to a nervous condition.

The Toughest Task ---- Ethics

What I Used to Think: You're either ethical or you're not.

Nobody Told Me: Being ethical is a choice you must make again and again. Moral standards, like other standards, can deteriorate. Sometimes the ethical path isn't readily apparent, and it's difficult to be sure you're doing the right thing. Sometimes social or business trends cloud your judgment.

Companies must establish and maintain ethical standards. To me, customer service is an issue of ethics. The reason why your business should give customers great service isn't because you will lose their business otherwise but because you have promised to deliver a product or a service in exchange for their money. I take good care of my customers, not because I've read a study that says angry customers tell more people about a bad experience than happy customers tell people about a good experience, but because it's the right thing to do and makes me feel good about my company.

Behaving ethically also comes into play in your relationships with employees and vendors. Being ethical doesn't mean you never fire employees. It means you tell them what you expect up front, treat all employees equally, and make no promises you may be unable to keep. Similar rules apply to vendors. How to stretch out your payables is a hot business topic now. I've heard speakers encourage audience members to delay paying their bills. How? In one case by telling vendors that their controller had to have surgery. My guess is, most business owners realize that it's unethical to stretch out a payable by lying. But they may begin to question what they know in their hearts is right after reading a few articles and hearing a few speeches by people who recommend the practice.

Paying your bills in a timely fashion is a matter of ethics, not business expediency. You need to determine ethical standards not by following trends but by following your own gut instincts. Someone who recently went into bankruptcy said to me, "Bankruptcy isn't the shameful thing it used to be. Now it's just a business strategy." I find that offensive. Bankruptcy may be a business strategy, but it's a last-ditch business strategy no one should take lightly.

If you're like me, you probably consider yourself an ethical person. No matter how ethical you think you are, though, there may be times when you're tempted to do what you know is wrong. A customer may accidentally send a double payment just when your company really could use the money. Do you put the money in your account and hope the customer doesn't notice, or do you return the check? It may be tempting to deposit the check, but the ethical thing to do in this case is very clear. You must return the check.

Sometimes ethical issues are not black and white. A man who sold photography lab services to large retail chains told me he also could supply frames to his clients. He offered to sell my company's frames for a commission. It seemed like a good opportunity for my company, but I decided to decline his offer. I realized that I wouldn't want my salaried employees selling someone else's products or services on my time and came to the conclusion that it would be unethical for me to go along with his scheme. I'm sure many employees and even some of their bosses would have no problem with this arrangement. Determining what is ethical can be somewhat subjective. Just be aware that when you're in business for yourself, you will run into these dilemmas on a regular basis.

Adopting high ethical standards is something you do for its own sake. Another nice thing about being ethical is that it pays. If you establish a strong code of ethics for your company and stick to them, you will have employees who are proud to work there, vendors who cherish your account, and customers who are loyal.

Lesson #25: Being ethical is a full-time job.

The Hymns of Mediocrity

What I Used to Think: Workers who are ones and twos on a scale from one to ten are my worst employee problem.

Nobody Told Me: Mediocre employees are more problematic than bad employees. Why? It's easy to fire the worst employees but difficult to fire mediocre employees. If you provide good training, a nurturing environment, and do everything else you can to help employees perform their jobs well, there's no good reason to hold onto employees who are just fives and sixes on a scale from one to ten. Ask yourself how you would feel if a given employee told you today that he/she were leaving. If you wouldn't feel sorry to lose that employee, he/she probably should be off your payroll. That's my litmus test.

Employers sing four hymns of mediocrity whenever they hold onto employees who are neither good nor bad, just in-between. "We could do worse" is the first one. Well, you know, you *always* can do worse. That's no reason to avoid doing something.

The second hymn is, "They try so hard." Trying hard may count in grade school, but your customers don't know or care how hard your employees try. You, therefore, have to focus on results. I'd rather have someone who does a good job without trying than someone who does a bad job when trying his/her best.

The third hymn is, "They're getting better." The question is, will they ever be good? In my experience, there's a point at which employees make few if any improvements, and you can usually tell if they've reached that point.

The fourth and last hymn of mediocrity is, "They've been here so long." I asked a group of business owners during a roundtable discussion what they do when a longtime employee no longer performs well on the job. Contrary to what people might think, they didn't shout in unison, "Fire the bum!" Instead, they shook their heads in misery because each of them had struggled or was struggling with that problem.

It's very difficult to fire someone who no longer performs their job well or never did. Some employers decide to carry these employees until they retire. I've done that with a few people, but I can't afford to do that with many of them. I've frozen their salaries, moved them into different positions, encouraged them to find work elsewhere, and, yes, fired them. You can't build a top-notch organization with employees who are fives and sixes. You also risk losing your best employees because they become frustrated working with the mediocre ones.

Lesson #26: The best place for mediocre employees is with the competition.

The Ultimate Quick-Change Artist

What I Used to Think: Your role as a business owner remains pretty much the same until you go into semi-retirement.

Nobody Told Me: Your role as a business owner constantly changes, especially as your company grows. Moreover, the appropriate role of the boss varies, depending on where your company is in terms of growth, your industry, and your personal strengths.

Like most business owners, I had to wear numerous hats when I first started my business. I also had to monitor my abilities and work hard to build my strength in those areas, like management, where I was weak. As my company grew, however, I hired a controller, sales manager, operations manager, and other professionals who oversee day-to-day operations. With those people in place, I had to shift gears. Instead of focusing on what I was bad at because it might kill my business, I had to figure out what my role should be based on my strengths. I took inventory of my skills to determine how I could be most useful to my company. I realized that marketing is my strong suit and now devote more energy to that area. By no means, however, do I neglect other areas.

Regardless of their personal strengths, owners in some industries have to be out there selling, developing new products, or doing whatever else is vital for the success of their businesses. Whatever the industry and whatever the developmental stage of your company, you have to continually ask yourself, "What's the most important thing for my company right now, and how can I best leverage my abilities in the service of my company?"

Lesson #27: Your job as a boss changes as much as your business does.

Have You Paid Your Dues Today?

What I Used to Think: Once you pay your dues, you can stop making so many sacrifices.

Nobody Told Me: You never finish paying your dues if you want to keep your business growing. You have to pay new dues every time you take your business to a higher plateau. Before you take your business to a new level, however, it's wise to figure out what the dues will be and whether you want to pay them. I have three framing showrooms in metropolitan Chicago, all of which are profitable, so I've considered franchising the business nationally. After researching franchises, however, I realized I would have to pay high dues for having out-of-state locations. I would have to spend a lot of time on airplanes and would have much less control of each franchise than I do of my own showrooms. I decided to forego franchising my business and the additional income it might generate because I didn't want to pay those particular dues.

I learned the phrase *utility of money* in accounting, and it applies to this lesson. According to this theory, your first million dollars is far more valuable to you than, say, your twelfth million. Once you have a comfortable lifestyle, money in the bank, and security, you're unlikely to consider it worthwhile to work twice as hard for twice as much money. As I grow my business, I continue to ask myself, "Do I want to work 50 percent harder or experience 50 percent more grief to make 50 percent more money?" After careful consideration, I have concluded that I don't need to be that rich. I earn enough money, and my business is growing steadily without my having to pay excessively high dues.

Lesson #28: You can't escape paying dues, but you may first be able to determine just how much you want to shell out.

Stop Being So Gullible

What I Used to Think: If they say it's so, it *must* be so.

Nobody Told Me: Don't believe everything people tell you. Some people flat out lie. Others just don't know what the hell they're talking about. When I was in my twenties and heard an older salesperson make a pitch by saying, "I've been doing this for 20 years," I was always impressed. Now a red flag goes up in my head whenever I hear that line. Everyone I've known whose only claim to fame is how long he/she has been doing something, has wound up being incompetent. I didn't realize when I was younger that there are people who do things wrong for 20 years or longer. I've learned age and experience aren't necessarily indicators of competency. There are 28-year-old workers who have better experience and are more competent than their 60-year-old counterparts.

I also had to learn that people can look you right in the eye and lie without so much as blinking. When you're an honest person, you assume other people are equally honest. When you say, "I'm going to be candid," you probably mean it. But that's a standard line some people use every day just before they tell a lie.

Lesson #29: No one ever says, "I'm about to lie to you. Here it comes."

A Little Ignorance Is Bliss in Business

What I Used to Think: You need to know every time your company screws up an order and personally discuss it with the customer.

Nobody Told Me: You can drive yourself nuts obsessing over every mistake and thinking you're the only one who can make things right. I attribute my company's success, in part, to my personal involvement early on in every aspect of the business, especially quality control and customer service. As my business expands, however, it's better for me to remain ignorant of some problems. Even if more than 99 percent of my customers are thrilled, once or twice a week a customer is dissatisfied. I still have time to get involved in customer problems and often do, but it's aggravating. It temporarily shatters my confidence in the company. I start thinking "Oh, my god, we screwed up. How can I even consider expansion." Now that I have several good managers on board and am confident of their ability to resolve problems, I realize that it's OK to let them have some of the aggravation. I don't have to take it all on myself.

Lesson #30: You can delegate some of the grief.

Just Say Yes to Stress

What I Used to Think: Stress is an occupational hazard only for air traffic controllers and high-powered corporate executives.

Nobody Told Me: Stress has been a part of life since cave-dwellers had to hunt for the family dinner. Stress has a negative connotation, and everyone is trying to eradicate stress in their lives. But job stress is a reality for most successful business professionals. For business owners, little compares to knowing there are people counting on you to make payroll at the end of every week. It's also unimaginably stressful to be aware that if one large receivable goes bad, your company may go out of business. As business owners, we frequently are just a few bad decisions away from going broke. Do you ever get used to it? Not entirely. The more money you earn, the more job stress you likely will have. Jobs without stress often pay significantly less than more stressful jobs.

When my employees start whining about how difficult their jobs are, I tell them the same thing. My sales consultants earn up to 100 percent more than their counterparts at other frame shops because they have more responsibility and, hence, more stress. I accept that I have to deal with stress if I expect to make a lot of money. I also accept that I have to pay higher wages to employees who have stressful jobs.

When you accept that stress is part of a typical business day, you're better able to take stressful events in stride. Accepting stress doesn't mean you stop trying to minimize and manage stress.

Lesson #31: $TRE$$ is spelled with dollar signs.

Why Johnny the Entrepreneur Doesn't Read

What I Used to Think: When one is busy supervising employees, he does not have time to read business magazines. Besides, there's nothing to learn from businesses outside your industry.

Nobody Told Me: It's cheaper to learn from other people's mistakes than from your own. You may think reading magazines at the office is a frivolous activity, but business magazines are important sources of ideas, inspiration, and lessons. Reading about other people's business experiences, their successes and failures, is a quick and easy way to pick up anecdotal information that can help you run your business better or avoid making critical mistakes. Growing businesses, no matter in what industry, face similar challenges. I gain perspectives on issues affecting my company when I read about other businesses dealing with similar issues.

Business magazines also help you keep up with legislation, the economy, and other overarching issues that may affect your business. You don't have to read every article, but if you fail to devote some time to reading business magazines, you're shutting yourself off from a valuable resource. I avoid magazines that strictly focus on business start-ups because they often contain a lot of hype. Instead, I seek out publications that focus on growing businesses. There also are audiotapes, videotapes, and conferences like those sponsored by the magazine *Inc.*

Lesson #32: You have to *make* time to read business magazines.

Part III – Management:

If You Want the Job Done Right, Be a Great Manager

What Employees Really Want

What I Used to Think: You have to develop sophisticated motivational programs if you want employees to love working for your company.

Nobody Told Me: The issue is *demotivation*, not motivation. Most people are naturally motivated until you scream at them a few times, put off their raise reviews for a few months, or continually neglect to tell them when they have done an exceptionally good job. Most people want to get behind something, whether it's a local sports team, their alma maters, or a radio personality. Why, I've often wondered, are they loathe to support the companies they work for at least forty hours a week? I contend it isn't that they're dissatisfied with their pay. Instead, they feel disenfranchised.

I give presentations at business conferences around the country. Members of the audience often ask me, "What can I do to get my employees to treat my business like it's their own?" Many of those persons are the same ones who lose their temper with employees, fail to keep employees informed, exclude them from decision-making processes, and do all of the other things that make people dislike their jobs. I tell them to stop looking for the magical motivational program and instead figure out what they're doing to demotivate employees.

I know a business owner who every year gave his employees a bonus but one year couldn't because business had been very slow. I asked him, "So, did you sit down with everyone and explain what happened?" He said, "No, I put a notice on the bulletin board." That's pathetic. No motivational program can undo the damage that kind of mismanagement does.

I use the acronym *FROSI* to help me remember what employees are looking for from their employers. *F* stands for *fairness,* which means you give raise reviews on time, make no unreasonable demands, and treat all employees equally. *R* stands for *respect,* which means you refrain from screaming at employees, let them know they're making a contribution, and instead of just telling them what to do, you explain why. *O* stands for *opportunity,* which means you provide as much upward mobility as possible to employees who consistently work hard and take the initiative. *S* stands for *security,* which means your employees know you never capriciously hire and fire people. I believe other employees deserve to know why a fellow employee has been fired as long as the privacy of the fired person is not compromised. Violation of attendance policy, substandard work, or low productivity are not private matters. If you don't explain what happened to other employees, they will be left to make assumptions which may be totally inaccurate. *I* stands for *inclusion,* which means you involve employees, when appropriate, in decision-making and keep them informed about how the company is doing and where it's going.

Lesson #33: Usually it's what we do wrong, not what we do right, that has the greatest impact on our companies.

Put Your Money Down on Wisdom

What I Used to Think: If you have talent, you can succeed in business.

Nobody Told Me: Talent may result in a big top line but may not necessarily result in a big bottom line. You can be talented at sales and even customer service, but it takes business smarts to translate those talents into profits. There are at least twenty expenses, from advertising and salaries to insurance and rent, that can eat your profits if you don't know how to control them. Likewise, talent won't prepare you for the changes that take place when your business grows. When my company first began growing, I assumed it also would become more profitable. As my customer volume increased, I thought I would get better volume discounts on materials and increase my profit margins. I was right about the volume discounts, but failed to foresee the extent to which my other costs would increase.

If your business is growing, you need adequate profit margins to cover the cost of growth. As you move from a one-person shop to a full-fledged business, you may become less efficient. There are more salaries to pay and higher insurance costs, among numerous other expenses. That's why it's easier to get a good deal from an independent house painter, for instance, than a house painting company.

When it comes to business savvy, most of us pick it up along the way. Unfortunately, the most common way to gain business smarts is by being in business for many years and making lots of mistakes. I think you can avoid making deadly mistakes. Understand that even though you may have a natural sales ability or a talent for developing new concepts, you have to focus a lot of energy on learning about business. It's always better to learn from other people's experiences than from your own mistakes. Find a mentor, join business organizations, and read periodicals. Above all, keep your eye on the bottom line.

Lesson #34: Talent may result in a big top line, but wisdom results in a big bottom line.

Forget about Being Number One

What I Used to Think: The best you can be is number one.

Nobody Told Me: In business it's better to be profitable than to be number one. There are many good analogies between business and sports. But being number one in business, unlike in sports, isn't always the best thing. A football team, for instance, can play a bad game and win the Super Bowl if the other team plays even worse. As long as the winning team has more points, they're number one. In business you can be number one and make little or no money. I'd rather be number seventy-three and make $1 million than be number one and make $100.

The goal of business is to optimize. If you optimize, you're more likely to be profitable. To increase my company's profitability, I try to attract as many customers as I can without sacrificing quality and without letting my expenses get out of control. The most profitable companies often are the best-run companies. The best-run companies often, but not always, are number one in their industries.

My company is the largest retail, custom picture-framing facility in the country. At times we have screwed up orders. At those times I could have said to myself, "We're still better on our worst day than our closest competitor is on their best day." I've always said, instead, "We have to do better. We have an obligation to do the job right. If we had done the job right, we would have made more money."

Lesson #35: Big sales figures feed big egos. Big profits feed big bank accounts.

In a Word ---- Systems

What I Used to Think: You have to be in control of your business, whatever that means.

Nobody Told Me: My father told me at least a hundred times, "You must have *control* of your business." It took years for me to fully understand what that means. As it turns out, control is neither as mysterious nor elusive as I had thought. Control boils down to two things: knowing what is going on and making sure what you want happen actually does.

Knowing what is going on means you have systems in place that give you the numbers you need. You know how much inventory you have, how much you sell each month, what your receivables are, and what your expenses are.

The other half of the equation is making sure what you want to happen actually does. That means you have to monitor your systems. I decided, for instance, that every finished frame job should come with a tag that reads, "Thank-you for your business." I could have told everyone what I wanted, but it would have made no difference unless I put a system in place and monitored it. That's why I made my sales consultants responsible for inspecting and affixing tags to finished pieces. If one of my employees responsible for customer pickups discovers a piece without a tag, he/she calls the sales consultant over to inspect and tag the piece.

Lesson #36: S-Y-S-T-E-M-S.

Improve Your Hiring Odds ---- Take a BATH

What I Used to Think: Hiring is a crapshoot.

Nobody Told Me: I realized that I had a serious management problem when my accountant observed that I had 80 W2 forms and only 30 employees. I continually hired and fired employees because I knew little about hiring and even less about management. I went through hundreds of employees before I figured out how to make a good hire. Hiring always carries some risk, but you can improve your odds by establishing the right criteria. Job requirements vary from job to job, but hiring criteria remain pretty much the same for every position. The right hiring criteria, however, vary depending on the personality and needs of your company.

After I noticed many similarities among my best employees, I established what I call the *BATH* test to help me spot the best prospective employees for my company. The *BATH* test is a set of questions we ask ourselves about all prospective employees.

"*B*" stands for do they *buy* into the concept? The concept in my company is outstanding customer service. We try to determine whether people will do everything within reason to make our customers happy.

"*A*" stands for are they *able?* To provide outstanding customer service, we must employ people who can do the job. We look for people who have proven track records in similar positions or personalities that are a good fit for both the job and my company.

"*T*" stands for are they *team* players? Team players aren't people who blindly go along with everyone else. I'm looking for employees who will actively participate in the company. They will follow procedures but will tell you if there is a problem with a procedure and suggest solutions. They will tell you *whatever* is on their minds, for that matter. Team players look out for the good of the company, not just themselves.

Lastly, "*H*" stands for are they *hungry?* A growing company thrives on employees who are hungry for success and eager to take advantage of any opportunity.

We take the *BATH* test seriously and don't hire people unless they meet all four criteria. I've shared the BATH test with other business owners, many of whom told me later that it has significantly improved their success in hiring.

Lesson #37: Hiring is more like a science than a crapshoot.

The Entrepreneur's Achilles' Heel

What I Used to Think: Good management dictates that the boss is the best person to do the hiring.

Nobody Told Me: If you're a typical entrepreneur, you may not be the best person to do the hiring at your company. When your business is small, you have to make all of the hiring decisions. As your company grows, you have to choose how involved you want to be in hiring.

It first occurred to me that someone else might have more talent for hiring than I do when I interviewed an experienced sales manager for a position at my company. I asked her how many people she had to fire at her previous job. She said, "I haven't had to fire anybody." I told her, "You either have lower standards than I do or you're some kind of hiring god." I hired her and soon discovered she *was* a hiring god. She has fired a few people at my place, but her success rate after two years is about 90 percent. My success rate was only about 65 percent.

Like most entrepreneurs, I have many distractions. So, I interview fewer prospects than I should and spend too little time with them. I also have a tendency to spend too much time talking about my company and too little time asking questions and listening to answers. Moreover, many entrepreneurs are salespeople. They like and trust people, so they usually excel at sales. They may not, however, possess the skepticism needed to make good hires.

Lesson #38: You could be the worst person to do the hiring at your company.

The Tilt-a-Whirl

What I Used to Think: Everyone likes working for a dynamic company.

Nobody Told Me: My business is like a tilt-a-whirl. The tilt-a-whirl is a carnival ride that has cup-shaped cars you sit in with four or five other people. The cars go 'round and 'round on a platform with tracks for each car. Sometimes the cars go 'round very slowly and sometimes they go 'round very fast. It's easy to tell who is enjoying the tilt-a-whirl and who isn't. The former look exhilarated and want the ride to last forever. The latter look scared out of their wits and can't wait to get back on firm ground. Same ride, different people. My business, like most growing businesses, provides employees with a dynamic working environment. One of my employees or I may have an idea, and within a few days the company could be gearing up to spin off a new business. Some people like that kind of excitement. Some don't.

It was very frustrating, for instance, trying to hire a controller many years ago for my company. There's a profound lack of structure inside a small, growing company. Deadlines and job descriptions are in constant flux. When I described the frenetic pace and the importance of versatility to prospective controllers, I could see how nervous it made them. I eventually found a controller who could relate to what I was saying. When she said the job was exactly what she was looking for, she meant it and has been with me ever since.

Lesson #39: Don't try to fit square pegs into round holes.

Taking Pains to Train Employees

What I Used to Think: Employee training is impractical for small companies. Besides, people learn best just by doing.

Nobody Told Me: It costs more *not* to train your employees than to train them. You can count on poorly trained employees making mistakes that will cost your company money. Their mistakes may irritate and even drive away customers. The employees also suffer.

No one likes to screw up. If you fail to train your employees, they're more likely to feel frustrated on the job and quit. I instituted training programs for my employees several years ago and have never looked back.

My sales consultants spend a month observing production employees before they even set foot on the sales floor. Sales consultants and production employees receive basic math training to make sure they understand fractions. They also receive training in how to measure. Most employees are too embarrassed to admit they don't know something as basic as how to take accurate measurements. Taking accurate measurements is critical in my business, so I can't take any chances. I train and test them until they know what they're doing. This way they never have to admit their ignorance, and we never have to wonder whether they have the knowledge and skills they need to do their job.

Sales consultants spend an additional month assisting experienced consultants before they help their first customers. The training helps my sales consultants feel more competent and earn higher commissions. They feel good about themselves and their jobs. Of course, our customers benefit.

I provide general training to other employees, including my receptionist and drivers. They learn how the company works so they can answer basic customer questions. It irritates me when I ask a receptionist a simple question, and he/she says, "I don't know. I'm just the receptionist." All employees need training, whether it's just shadowing an experienced employee for a few weeks or undergoing formal instruction.

Lesson #40: Well-trained employees are worth the cost in training expenses, no matter what size your company.

For, Against, and Best of All, With

What I Used to Think: Employees either work for or against you.

Nobody Told Me: There's a third category of employees whom you need to identify and foster: those who work *with* you. Before we get to them, however, let's simplify this lesson by addressing the problem of employees who work against you. Employees who work *against* you shouldn't be working for you. Get rid of them.

That leaves employees who really work for you and those who work with you. "Work-fors" know what they're supposed to do and do it, but are unlikely to alert you to problems or let you know when they're unhappy. "Work-withs" do what they're supposed to do and also understand the company's mission, feel responsible for the company's overall well-being, and tell you what is going on.

A man who works on my dock pulled me over several years ago and said, "Keep an eye on the new guy. I'm not sure, but I think he slipped something of ours into his pocket." He is a work-with. A work-for never says anything because they don't want to get involved.

Both kinds of employees are valuable to your organization, but you need to identify who is who and treat each one accordingly. All employees who report directly to you should be work-withs. They will not only tell you what they're thinking but they also can handle it when you tell them what is on your mind. If you treat work-fors like work-withs, they may feel overwhelmed. If you treat work-withs like work-fors, they may feel insulted. Not everybody has to be a work-with, but you should recognize that work-withs are valuable assets to your company. Identify them and foster their growth. They will keep you in close touch with your company, watch your back, and go the extra mile.

Lesson #41: Work-withs are a blessing.

Don't Try to Make a Cow Fly, Either

What I Used to Think: If you just nurture your employees enough, they will blossom.

Nobody Told Me: There's more than a little truth to the old saying, "don't try to make a pig sing. You won't succeed, and you'll irritate the pig."

I used to have great aspirations for some employees. Two young guys who worked for me when I first started my business stand out in my mind. I remember saying to myself, "I'm really going to nurture these guys. I'm going to train and educate them, and they're going to grow with me and the company." It was a hard lesson, but I eventually realized that these kids didn't want the same things I wanted for them. I wanted them to take on more responsibility, make more money, and move up in the world, but they were happy being at the bottom and staying there. That's where their friends were, and that's where their friends wanted them to stay. It was heart-wrenching for me, but I finally had to give up on these guys.

Sometimes I succeed at lifting employees up. In this case I failed. You can't make employees into people they don't want to be. You may have the best intentions, but your employees may think, "Why is he all over my ass all the time?" In the case of these two guys, I was wasting my time. One could even argue I was unfair to them.

Lesson #42: Some employees don't want to improve themselves. Everyone is not like you.

Open-Book Management 101

What I Used to Think: Employees understand your expenses.

Nobody Told Me: Your employees most likely will assume that you're making an obscene profit on everything you do unless you tell them otherwise.

I developed a demonstration that I call "Showing Where the Money Goes" to help employees understand the fiscal realities of this business. I want them to understand that the dollar amount they see on our invoices doesn't wind up in my pocket. More importantly, I want them to play a more active role in ensuring the company's profitability and keeping their jobs secure. I'm horrified when I hear about employees who are laid off after twenty years and have no idea why their companies went down the tubes.

How do you get complex business principles across, however, to a group of 110 employees who are as diverse as the world? Not every employee has a background in business administration. Not every company can afford to educate employees in how to read financial statements. Some of my employees have no education beyond high school. Others have college degrees in subjects ranging from fine art to engineering.

"Showing Where the Money Goes" is a fun, interactive, easy-to-understand, and practical way to show employees how expensive running a business is and why everyone must take responsibility for keeping down costs. I give this demonstration every year as part of a company-wide meeting.

I call on a manager to play the role of a customer with a $100 framing job. The manager, equipped with oversized play money, pays for the framing job dollar by dollar as I spell out the expenses that went into it. "What do you think it costs to run one of our display ads in the Yellow Pages?" I ask the audience. Employees shout out answers ranging from $100 to $2,000. They're are shocked when I tell them the monthly charge for a display ad is $3,000. Marketing, I tell them, eats 5 percent of every framing job. My make-believe customer hands over $5. I go down the entire list of expenses, including workmen's compensation, materials, salaries, the works, collecting money from my "customer" each step of the way.

At the very end of the demonstration, there are just $4 or $5 left, and that's before taxes. So now we're talking about just a couple of bucks. Whatever your profit, it's probably a lot less than your employees think. My employees enjoy and learn from the presentation. It helps them understand that the difference between success and failure is just a few percentage points. It also shows how their jobs and salaries fit into the big picture.

Lesson #43: If you want your employees to understand your business, you have to educate them.

A Word about Empowerment

What I Used to Think: Everyone is talking about empowerment. It must be a good thing.

Nobody Told Me: *Empowerment* is a complex concept that has been reduced to a buzzword. You can't empower employees without initially giving them a lot of guidance. You never should empower some employees. Empowerment is a legitimate concept many people fail to fully understand. It's wise to empower some employees but foolish to empower others. Some employees are very good at what they do but have poor judgment. They're no good at troubleshooting. Likewise, some employees collapse under the pressure of having to make decisions or feel devastated if they make the wrong decisions.

That's why you have to be careful about whom you empower and how much you empower them. There's a difference between empowering a vice president to make important decisions affecting the company and empowering loading dock personnel to reject shipments in damaged boxes.

I empower my sales consultants, for example, to handle a wide range of customer problems. This works beautifully. They feel better about themselves, and I don't have to be summoned every time there's a problem. That allows me to concentrate on new business opportunities, and it makes the company look good.

Before empowering my sales consultants, I give them examples of how to resolve specific customer problems. If there's a quality control problem, for instance, we offer to redo the job. If it is inconvenient for a customer to pick up the new order, we offer free delivery. If we screw up and can't have someone's picture ready for a party, we offer to loan the customer another picture. If we run out of the framing materials a customer has ordered, we offer to frame the picture in another style and reframe it with the material the customer originally wanted as soon as possible.

You can say to your employees, "Hey, I'm empowering you." But it means nothing unless you give them some guidance and help them develop the skills and experience necessary to take on the added responsibility.

Lesson #44: You can turn little problems into big problems by empowering the wrong people.

Loose Cannons

What I Used to Think: Everyone blows his top once in a while.

Nobody Told Me: What you say in anger can cause irreparable damage, not only to the person who is the target of your anger but also to your company. When people are angry, they often engage in character assassination. I heard one of my managers say to a tardy employee, "You obviously don't care about your job." Well, that's inaccurate and what I call a "blanket" indictment. If someone is late, it's appropriate to say, "You were late this morning. If you're late again, we're going to put you on probation."

I no longer let employees get away with making indictments because they're unfair and detract from identifying real problems and their solutions. When one of my managers said to me, "That receptionist's such an idiot," I asked, "What do you mean by that?" She said, "I was paging somebody who had left the building, and the receptionist never told me she was gone." I replied, "Are you sure she knew that the person had left the building? Is it possible that even if she did know, she was unaware that it was her responsibility to inform you? Instead of telling me she's an idiot, why not just ask her to please tell you when someone you're paging has left the building?"

I also question employees when they indict customers. I often hear them say a customer is "crazy" when in reality the customer is unhappy because we screwed up an order. Sometimes we do everything right, and customers still are unpleasant either because that's their nature or they're having a bad day. That doesn't mean they're crazy. Indictments, by definition, are unproved. They serve no purpose in business. Simple statements of fact, on the other hand, are very useful. They help you identify real problems and their solutions.

Lesson #45: Leave indictments to the attorney general.

Cutting Slack

What I Used to Think: Employees know you won't hold it against them if they occasionally make a mistake.

Nobody Told Me: An employee who makes a mistake may assume you're angry about it unless you tell him/her otherwise. There's a difference between poor performance and an accident. You should hold employees who continually make mistakes responsible for their poor performance. You should let employees off the hook who consistently perform well but have an occasional accident.

A very conscientious employee who puts pictures together at my company dropped glass on a signed photograph, causing serious damage. The photograph was worth about $2,000. I obviously wasn't happy when I heard about it but figured she probably felt worse than I did. I made a beeline to her workstation and said, "You're one of the most careful fitters we have here. I know you're upset about this. It was an accident, and accidents are just a cost of doing business." There's nothing to be gained by screaming at employees who make an occasional mistake or standing by while they eat themselves up with guilt or embarrassment. I don't want my employees to be up all night worrying that I'm angry at them.

Lesson #46: Letting employees off the hook for occasional accidents is worth as much as a thousand "attaboys."

Mo' Meetings

What I Used to Think: Meetings are a waste of time. They just keep people from working.

Nobody Told Me: Meetings are a critically important management tool that can radically improve your employees' productivity. I ran into a lot of quality control problems shortly after my business took off. Too many employees weren't doing what they were supposed to do. Jobs were going out half-assed. I hired a big consulting firm to provide some answers. Several fresh-faced MBAs spent three weeks at my business and prepared a massive report full of charts and graphs. I pored over the report, for which I shelled out about $10,000, and found nothing of value.

It was extremely frustrating, but a few months later I tried again. I hired an independent consultant, Monroe Roth, who had worked as a company president. After our second meeting, he wrote a one-paragraph letter that summed up the problem and helped me change the course of my business. He observed that I was failing to manage my managers. I was treating them, instead, like CEOs.

I immediately instituted weekly managers' meetings, which are invaluable for discussing and solving problems, keeping people informed, brainstorming ideas, and keeping people on schedule. We identify and solve problems more quickly now because the meetings provide a venue for addressing problems and more people are involved in the problem-solving process.

I remember discussing business problems with a group of business owners many years ago and inwardly laughing when one guy said that his biggest problem was communication. I said to myself, "What do you mean, *communication?* Yell louder!" I just didn't understand it back then. I now know communication is very important and can't be taken for granted. People feel frustrated and excluded when you fail to keep them informed. I make sure my managers tell each other what they're doing to prevent them from duplicating or interfering with each other's efforts. I also make sure they always know my vision for the business as well as what is happening on a day-to-day basis.

As far as brainstorming goes, it's a great way not only to come up with new ideas but also to get employees more involved in the company. One of the greatest benefits of our weekly managers' meetings is keeping people on schedule. We establish timetables for getting work done. Managers are expected to report on their progress at each meeting. These progress reports create a powerful incentive for managers to get their work done in a timely fashion.

I eventually instituted weekly sales meetings and various department meetings. In sales meetings, our consultants learn about new products and new procedures. In department meetings, we emphasize problem solving. We review problems from the previous week, which usually fall into the categories of performance, procedures, or planning. We determine the source of each problem and brainstorm solutions. Before we instituted department meetings, my employees just treated the symptoms, never asking themselves what the root causes of problems were.

Lesson #47: Big companies have too many meetings. Small companies have too few.

Hot on the Problem Trail

What I Used to Think: Problems just happen. You deal with them as you go along.

Nobody Told Me: Most problems occur repeatedly for a reason. I introduced *hot tickets* to help us quickly resolve problems. I soon found out they also help us track problems. Once you identify recurrent problems, you can start looking for causes and finding solutions.

Hot tickets are an integral part of my business. Our success rate is more than 99 percent, meaning we have to redo roughly one of every 100 framing jobs. There are at least twenty things that can go wrong with every framing job. To develop our hot tickets, I created a checklist of these things. A salesperson may write down the wrong material on an invoice. A production employee may misread an invoice and use the wrong material. There may be a quality control problem such as dirt under the glass or a scratch on the moulding. Maybe the art has been placed the wrong way in the frame because the instructions were unclear. Maybe the job wasn't ready when it was supposed to be. Sometimes we do everything right but the customer still is unhappy. Maybe the customer selected a blue mat but doesn't like the way it looks on the finished piece.

Our sales consultants inspect every finished piece. If a sales consultant or customer finds a problem, the sales consultant fills out a hot ticket. The consultant checks off the cause or causes of the problem and notifies the production staff that a job must immediately be redone.

I tell employees how important it is to take the time to accurately fill out hot tickets. Hot tickets help ensure that problems with framing jobs are resolved quickly.

They also tell us what problems are recurring. We monitor the hot tickets at the end of every week. If the wrong moulding is pulled five times in one week, for instance, we know where to begin our investigation. Maybe the person pulling the moulding is goofing off. Maybe they can't see the numbers on the shelves because the lighting is poor, the numbers are too small, or there are two mouldings with similar numbers right next to each other.

There are dozens of reasons why people make mistakes. Hot tickets help us find the root causes of our most frequent mistakes. We learned after several months of monitoring hot tickets that customers frequently complained about the positioning of their art in the mat or frame. We realized a few months later that the problem stemmed from art that is printed unevenly. We now position such art unevenly in the mat or frame so that it appears straight.

Lesson #48: Problems have specific causes and specific solutions. Make sure you have systems in place to track them.

Happy Families Aren't Born ----
They're Assembled

What I Used to Think: Your company will be like one big happy family if you nurture and treat everyone fairly.

Nobody Told Me: If you want to have a warm, wonderful company, you have to do some cold, unpleasant things. I remember watching an awards presentation on television for a highly successful company. An employee came to the podium to accept an award. Weeping, she said, "I love working here. You're all like family to me. I love you so much." I was having all sorts of management problems at the time. I just thought to myself, "What am I doing wrong? Everybody at this company is so happy. Everything is family this and family that. How come I don't have that?"

A few years later, I was talking to someone who worked for that same company and learned that when they fire or lay off someone they have a security guard escort that employee out the door. No one mentioned the security guard at the awards presentation. That's when I realized to create a warm, wonderful company, you have to be highly selective about whom you hire and keep on staff.

If you nurture your employees, many of them will act and feel like they're part of a family. I can walk into work on any given day and see employees who are excellent at their jobs, proud of the company, and ready to help me meet any challenge. We provide each other moral support. It's a wonderful feeling.

There also are employees who appreciate the family environment your company fosters but are incompetent. Other employees resent having to work with them. Employees who fail to work out, for whatever reason, usually quit. Sometimes I have to fire them. I guess one of the main differences between a company and a family is that you can't fire your relatives no matter how bad they are.

Lesson #49: Your company can be like one big happy family if you choose your "family members" well.

If You Want to Coddle Something, Get a Puppy

What I Used to Think: If an employee can't manage to get to work on time, buy the person an alarm clock.

Nobody Told Me: If you want to baby-sit, open a day care center. You can waste a tremendous amount of time and money on your worst employees to the detriment of your good employees and your business. At my company we tell employees what we expect of them from the start. If they fail to follow the rules or live up to our expectations, we discuss it with them once or twice but no more than that.

I had an employee who was chronically late to work. Week after week, I spent twenty minutes listening to excuses or arguing about whether 9:01 A.M. really is late before I realized I just couldn't afford the time. There are too many customers to take care of, too many problems to solve, and too many opportunities to explore to waste time baby-sitting employees who never will get it.

Lesson #50: You can't take over the world and baby-sit at the same time.

Check Your Mercy at the Door

What I Used to Think: You always should give employees a second chance.

Nobody Told Me: Second chances are fine, but there comes a time when someone has to be fired. You have to be compassionate but unmerciful when firing employees. Being compassionate means you fire people in private and let them go with their self-esteem intact. You may be angry at them, but there's no use letting off steam at this point. If you feel some personal responsibility for their well-being, provide a generous severance package. If you're hesitant to fire some-one—perhaps because the employee has been with you for years—keep the person in a position where the employee can do no harm.

After you give an employee adequate warning and deter-mine that the termination is appropriate, being unmerciful means you stick to your guns. I once had a forty-year-old man sob for ten minutes and beg me to give him another chance. I felt for him, but as a business decision, it was time for him to go. In life it's admirable to be merciful, but in business it can be unwise. If an order is late because an employee is upset over a personal matter, for instance, no customer will say, "That's OK. I understand." If unhappy customers give their business to a competitor, no competitor will say, "Hey, why don't you give Jay another chance? He is having a tough time." Capitalism, like nature, is both beautiful and cruel.

Lesson #51: You have to be less merciful than you'd like to be in the business world.

Wearing the Coroner's Hat

What I Used to Think: If employees don't work out, you can just fire them and forget them.

Nobody Told Me: Autopsies aren't just for dead bodies. My company's hiring record has improved dramatically since we instituted fire-and-quit-autopsies. We used to fire half of all new employees. Now we seldom have to fire anyone, and few employees quit. To do an "autopsy," I mean to take some time to figure out what went wrong and how you could have prevented it. Hiring good long-term employees is one of the best things you can do for your company, so it's crucial to understand why some employees didn't work out. Employees usually have to be fired or quit for one of two reasons. The first is, you made a bad hire. The second is, you made a good hire but the person left anyway. Maybe the employee decided to change careers, move away from the area, or just didn't fit in, and there was no way you could have predicted it.

There's little you can do about the second possibility, but what you learn from the first possibility is crucial. I usually can determine what went wrong by doing an autopsy. I may have waited until I was desperate before I began the hiring process and then failed to interview enough prospects and thoroughly screen the ones whom I did interview. I've conned myself into believing some people would be good hires because I got tired of interviewing people, liked their personalities, or only heard the answers I wanted to hear and missed clues from their references.

Now I assume everything a prospective hire tells me may be a lie. No one comes in and says, "I'm not that great of an employee. I'm pretty lazy, actually, and I always fight with my managers." No, the applicant says, "I'm a hard worker, and I'll do a great job for you." I discovered from doing autopsies that I could have predicted half of all bad hires during the interview process.

Lesson #52: If you fail to do fire-and-quit-autopsies, your business may wind up in the morgue.

The Time-Clock Mentality

What I Used to Think: If you put employees on salary, they will behave like salaried professionals.

Nobody Told Me: Some people need to be on the clock. I didn't have a time clock when I first started my business. Then I got a clock and put everybody on it. A little while later, I hired my first manager and put him on salary. After that I began to hire people who fell into that gray area. They could be classified as exempt employees but were neither managers nor production workers. I was unsure whether to put them on the clock or on salary. I decided to put them on salary because I thought it would make them feel like they were part of my company's management team and behave like salaried professionals. I was wrong. Some of them understood being on salary has both more advantages and responsibilities than being on the clock. They realized that even though they had to work late some nights without overtime, there were other benefits like paid sick days. Others, however, just didn't get it.

I put one employee on salary who had been an accountant in her native country. She held a position of responsibility before immigrating to this country, so I thought it would be insulting to put her on the clock. She flew out the door every day at 5:00 P.M. One morning after she failed to finish some work her manager needed the previous night, the manager asked, "Why didn't you stay late last night to finish your work?" The woman replied, "If I stay late, I miss my train, and the next one doesn't come for a long time." Her manager and I discussed the problem and decided to put her on the clock.

She immediately began to stay late whenever necessary. I guess the train schedule changed. I'm sure she would have been better off on salary, but she thought she was coming out ahead with time and a half. So it worked out best for both of us.

I now think long and hard before I put employees on salary. I make sure that they have been on salary at other jobs, or if they haven't, that they understand the benefits and accept the responsibilities of being on salary. I don't want people on salary who feel cheated if they have to work late now and then.

Lesson #53: When in doubt, put employees on the clock. You can always put them on salary after they have proved themselves.

Say Good-bye to the Super-Executive of Your Dreams

What I Used to Think: There has to be somebody out there who can run your business as well as you do.

Nobody Told Me: The typical entrepreneur holds numerous jobs. Unless you can afford to pay big bucks for a seasoned CEO, you will be lucky to find a person who can take over just one or two of your functions. When my business started growing, I often dreamed about that one person who could run the company while I brought in new business or just spent some time with my family. I never found anyone because I couldn't afford to pay the kind of money the market commands for someone with those abilities. Regardless of how much I can afford to pay someone, I've realized that the alternative is hiring several managers to take responsibility for several aspects of my job rather than one super-executive to do everything. It's just easier to find one person who is good at one job than one person who is good at three jobs.

Lesson #54: You may be better off without the super-person you're looking for to run your business. There's a name for those types. It's "entrepreneur."

Less-Is-More Management

What I Used to Think: It's the boss's job to tell everybody what to do.

Nobody Told Me: You undermine your managers, confuse employees, and cause other problems for yourself and your business when you micromanage your employees. You have to monitor everything your employees do when your company is young. But as soon as you hire your first manager, you have to learn how to hold your tongue. When you put managers in place at your organization, you establish a chain of command. You break the chain of command when you play the role of manager to lower-level employees.

I've learned to resist the temptation to jump in every time I see an employee do something wrong. I say something, instead, to the employee's manager. You create problems for yourself, your managers, and employees if you fail to follow that simple rule. Employees may get confused if you tell them one thing and their manager tells them something else. Moreover, your managers can't follow up with employees to make sure they're doing what you told them to do if they don't know that you told them to do something. The most destructive aspect of your interference, however, is that it demoralizes your managers. It undermines their authority, taking away some of their responsibility away and placing it on you.

Lesson #55: Manage your managers, but let them manage the rest of your employees.

The Open-Door Delusion

What I Used to Think: If you institute an open-door policy, everyone will feel free to talk to you.

Nobody Told Me: Just because you have an open door, don't expect your employees to feel comfortable walking through it. I used to read about corporate executives with open door policies and think to myself, "Man, how can a guy with 4,000 employees have an open-door policy? There must be a long line outside his office." I failed to see that the more employees you have, the less likely it is any of them will just drop by your office. People are intimidated by the boss. If you think announcing an open-door policy is going to change that, you're kidding yourself.

If you want to be in control of your business and know what is going on with your employees, go to them. Making the rounds and talking to employees is one of the most important ways I manage my business. I not only find out about problems this way but also prevent them. My business is located in a four-story, 35,000 square-foot warehouse. I'm sure some employees have no idea where my office is. I could sit and wait until the cows come home and never hear from or learn anything about my employees on the third floor.

I also have found that the car is a great place to find out what is going on with your employees. People laugh when I tell them a car is like a truth chamber, but it's true. Employees are unlikely to walk into your office and say, "So-and-so really doesn't work very hard" or "I've been thinking about going back to school" or "You know what really bothers me about this company?"

I regularly drive to meetings, seminars, and other functions with employees and have noticed that people say things to me in the car that they would never say to me in my office.

There are several reasons for this phenomenon, one of which is there's no agenda. Another reason people open up to you is that you're sitting side by side rather than face-to-face. The environment is intimate but nonthreatening. People also are just in the habit of having casual conversations in cars. That's what they do with their friends and family members. I'm not suggesting that you just take employees for drives. But if you want to get to know an employee better or have something you've been wanting to discuss with a particular employee, consider offering the person a lift to your next meeting.

Lesson #56: If you want to know what is going on in your company, institute a no-door policy. Don't wait for employees to walk through your "open" door.

The Ma, Pa, Sister Dorothy, and Cousin Seymour Shop

What I Used to Think: The best-run business is a family business because family members look out for each other. All or most of the key players have a personal stake in the company's success.

Nobody Told Me: If the happiness scale for a typical business is 1 to 10, then family businesses have to be rated on a scale from -10 to +20. A family business can be a living hell or heaven on earth for employees, vendors, and customers.

Parents unable to relinquish control of the day-to-day operation of their business to children or children who are unable to handle the responsibilities of working in the family business are among the most common problems. My three sons are too young to join my company, but I'm trying to prepare myself for the day when they may decide to come on board. I've been exposing them from an early age to the realities of the business world. I bring them to work on weekends and during their school holidays. I do whatever I can to help them understand the importance of treating other employees, customers, and vendors with respect. I'm aware, however, that children who come into family businesses may not be assets to those businesses.

I brought a cousin into the business many years ago. He worked out beautifully. My cousin had a strong work record, including managerial experience. He started out as a manager and worked his way up to vice president. He worked hard, proved himself competent, and earned the respect of his coworkers. From this experience I learned that you have to be careful about which relatives you bring into your company. I didn't hire my cousin as a favor to him or anyone else. I first made sure he fit the criteria I have established for new hires.

I also learned that it's imperative for your employees to feel as comfortable registering complaints against your relatives as they do against other employees. You could have a relative working for you and never hear how much they're teeing off your other employees and messing up your business. No one wants to tell the boss, "Your son is a brat. He just told Jack to get lunch for him." If you think it would be too difficult for your employees to speak up about a relative on the payroll, designate a trusted manager to monitor the situation.

You also can have nepotism at a company without ever hiring a single member of your own family. Many of my employees have brothers, sisters, children, or parents who work here. Good employees seldom ask you to interview a relative unless they're pretty sure that person will be an asset to your company. Many of my most competent, hardworking, and loyal employees are related. But I avoid having family members report to each other. I also make sure everyone understands from the start that relatives are held to the same standards as other employees and could be fired if they fail to meet those standards. Yes, it's difficult to fire a good employee's sister. But the benefits of hiring relatives of good employees far outweigh the disadvantages.

Lesson #57: There's a reason why hundreds of psychologists make good money counseling family businesses.

Setting Your Sights on Cupid

What I Used to Think: Employee romances are none of my business.

Nobody Told Me: There are only a few things more destructive to your business than office romances. It makes no difference whether the persons involved are high-level executives or maintenance workers. That's why I have an unwritten policy discouraging intimate relationships between employees.

The problem goes far beyond what happens when these relationships fail and the employees feel uncomfortable seeing each other at work every day. Office romances can disrupt an entire company. An infinite number of destructive scenarios could develop. The most serious problems arise when a manager has a relationship with a subordinate. It's nearly impossible to objectively manage someone to whom you're romantically attached. Moreover, managers risk crossing the line of sexual harassment when they pursue romances with subordinates. They also are vulnerable to false charges of sexual harassment should the relationship sour.

Problems arise even when two employees of equal rank are involved. Say two employees working in the same department have a relationship. The boyfriend is responsible for assigning framing orders to the other framers in the department. Maybe he starts giving the easiest framing orders to his girlfriend. The other employees notice and begin to resent it. Or maybe no one knows that these two employees are involved. A coworker bad-mouths the boyfriend to his girlfriend. The girlfriend tells the boyfriend and both of them shun the coworker who made the comment. Office romances, in general, create a tangled web of hurt feelings, inappropriate behavior, and resentment. You probably have seen the worst-case scenario on the news. The angry husband of an employee having an affair with a coworker shows up at his spouse's company with a semi-automatic rifle.

Written policies prohibiting office romances can be challenged in court, so I don't recommend including one in your employee manual. I explain to my managers that office romances are detrimental to the company, and they pass that information along to the rest of our employees. An unwritten policy discouraging office romances may lack the teeth of a written policy, but it may create social pressures that keep office romances to a minimum.

Lesson #58: M.Y.O.B. doesn't necessarily apply to office romances.

That Worker with the Pink Slip May Be Your Next Great Hire

What I Used to Think: You find new hires by placing help wanted ads.

Nobody Told Me: Companies that are downsizing, going out of business, or relocating are among your best resources for finding reliable, long-term production employees. These companies may have numerous stable employees who most likely have nothing to do with their employers' problems.

I contact the human resources managers of these companies and ask them for the names of employees who are losing their jobs. They're happy to assist because it helps them keep down their unemployment tax rate. Some failing companies even take a proactive stance and try to place employees with former competitors. They may have a social conscience or just view it as cost-effective.

I hired a few good employees from a company that was relocating. They, in turn, directed me to other employees they knew were hardworking and reliable. Most of these employees still are with my company and probably will be for a long time. You do, however, have to be careful to avoid hiring another employer's problems. I've had some failures using this approach. By and large, however, it's among the most successful hiring methods I employ.

Lesson #59: Great employees get handed pink slips every day. You may just want to put some of those folks back to work.

Creative Hiring

What I Used to Think: Hiring is finding the right person for the job.

Nobody Told Me: *Hiring* sometimes is finding the right job for the person. Great employees are hard to find, so if we come across an outstanding prospect, we try to leverage their abilities to the best of our ability.

Sometimes I hear about outstanding candidates through word of mouth. Sometimes they respond to help wanted ads. Some may not be right for the available position, but they're just too talented to let get away. We have created new positions and even shuffled the job responsibilities of employees to get a great prospect on board. I do whatever I can to find a place in my company for talented professionals.

I also look for great hires all the time, not just when I have openings. Some of your best prospective employees already have jobs. Their employers like them, and they like their employers. Most people, however, are interested in better opportunities, whether that means more money, a higher-level position, or a more desirable job location. Many successful companies actively recruit all the time. There's no good reason to limit your pool of candidates to those who are looking for a job.

Finally, it's not uncommon to struggle over *when* to hire your next employee. I believe it depends on the nature of the position. If the position is in production or customer service, you need to hire before it becomes a problem; take action before you lose customers because of your inability to serve them. If the position is in sales, you need to hire them when you can afford the negative cash flow resulting from the start-up phase. If you wait too long, you may lose customers or opportunities. If you hire too soon, you may lose money you can't afford to lose.

Lesson #60: Hiring is a creative process.

Unless You're Clairvoyant, Check References

What I Used to Think: No one is going to tell you anything about prospective employees that you can't figure out from interviewing them yourself. Besides, it's just too time consuming to check references.

Nobody Told Me: Whatever time you or your managers spend checking references is time well spent. It just costs too much money to make bad hires these days.

Prospective employees may give fraudulent references, but you never will know they're fraudulent unless you try calling them. Some people may go so far as setting up fraudulent phone lines. You call their references, get an answering machine, and leave a message. Your prospective employee's friends, posing as former employers, return your calls and give glowing references. You can be pretty sure someone who goes to these lengths to hoodwink you is after more than a job. I know because that's how I wound up with an embezzler in my accounting office. I lost some money, but it could have been worse. At any rate, it was a painful experience I never will forget. In hindsight, I could have called the phone company to verify that the phone numbers of the references he gave were valid. It was later I realized that all his reference information was phony.

I read about another case in which an newly-hired accountant stole blank checks from a company, stopped sending out payables, and then forged a check for a large amount to a phony account. The bank balance went up because of all the payable checks not clearing. By the time vendors started calling, the accountant had quit. The point is, checking references might have prevented this situation.

As far as legitimate references are concerned, some employers are very forthright when talking about former employees. These days, however, most companies have policies prohibiting human resources staff from giving references. Still, it's hard to believe that if an employee is really wonderful, someone wouldn't tell you so. I always ask, "Would you hire this person again?" Usually the person tells me it's against company policy to re-hire former employees, so I push just a little more by asking, "Well, what if it weren't against company policy?" If there's a long, awkward silence, chances are that employee hasn't been missed.

I suppose it's possible that every company someone's worked for is so afraid of liability no one will say anything, good or bad. I'm hesitant, however, to hire someone who is unable to provide me with one solid reference.

Lesson #61: Don't hire anyone, not even someone to sweep your sidewalks, without checking references.

Put on Your Gumshoe

What I Used to Think: Criminal background checks are only for hiring security guards and school bus drivers.

Nobody Told Me: There are a lot of people applying for jobs who have rap sheets and could be a serious threat to you, your company, and your employees. My company does background checks on all prospective employees. We use a firm that does a variety of checks including criminal, motor vehicle, social security, credit, and job references.

I used to believe everyone who said he/she never was convicted of a felony until I discovered one of them had a rap sheet as long as my arm. I might consider hiring someone who made some mistakes when they were young, served their time, and is rehabilitated. If they lie about it, that's another story. Some employers understand if applicants lie about their criminal records because they're afraid they won't get jobs if they tell the truth, but that's very risky. I want to know whether someone has had any criminal convictions, what they are, and the surrounding circumstances.

Prospective employees have an opportunity to reveal criminal records on their applications. We let them know we do background checks and ask them to sign an authorization form. If they don't want to submit to background checks, they don't have to, and I don't have to hire them. If they don't like the way I hire, they can apply for employment elsewhere.

Lesson #62: Like it or not, when you're the boss, you're held responsible for the actions of your employees. Know who you're hiring, not just who they *say* they are.

Putting New Hires to the Test

What I Used to Think: Testing prospective employees is more trouble than it's worth.

Nobody Told Me: You can waste a lot of time and money on the wrong employees. Pre-employment testing not only can save you tremendous grief but also can help you develop effective employee training. I give prospective employees personality tests and, depending on what position they're applying for, basic math tests.

The personality tests we use are very accurate. Before I instituted employee testing, I asked one of my employees to take the personality test so that we might gauge its accuracy. We read over the results. With a perfectly straight face she said, "The only thing that bothers me about this test is, it says I take criticism too personally." It was true, and her response confirmed it. She often became defensive whenever anybody told her she had done something wrong.

I never base hiring decisions solely on personality tests. But they help me leverage a new hire's personality strengths and help avoid putting people in situations where their personalities might cause problems. The tests often verify my suspicions about prospects and predict trouble spots. When those trouble spots flare up, I can quickly identify the source and take appropriate action.

The basic math tests also have proved to be a useful tool at my company. Our framing sales consultants, art consultants, production employees, and even installers have to take lots of measurements and do numerous calculations every day. Basic math tests tell me up front how much training new hires need. If their math skills are weak, and I have to do a lot of training, I may start them off at a lower pay scale than I would if they were coming in with those skills.

Lesson #63: You flunk if you don't do employee testing.

Just Say Yes to Drug Testing

What I Used to Think: It's pretty obvious when someone is on drugs.

Nobody Told Me: Drug users come from all walks of life and often are experts at hiding their habit. A drug user might be a suburban mother, a kid from the inner city, or a middle-aged man who has worked for the same company for twenty years.

Drug users can create all sorts of problems for you, your employees, and your company. They may buy and sell drugs on the premises. Their judgment may be impaired, resulting in accidents and difficulty getting along with other employees and customers.

When I place help wanted ads, I mention that we do drug testing. It helps screen out people who do drugs. Some people come in to fill out an application anyway, go through the interview process, and then back out when they realize that we're serious about drug testing. With more and more companies requiring drug tests, more and more drug users are gravitating to companies that don't test. I don't want them working for me.

I know there are people who think employee drug testing is an invasion of privacy, but given the level of liability business owners are subject to today, I strongly believe employers have to protect themselves. I don't want to trample on anyone's rights, but rights always must be balanced in a democracy. I have the right to run a safe company.

Lesson #64: You may not know if prospective employees are on drugs, but you will find out soon enough if you hire them.

Don't Orientate ---- Indoctrinate

What I Used to Think: New hires learn about your company as they go along.

Nobody Told Me: That could take a long time. I want them to get with the program right away, so I *indoctrinate* them. I give a presentation to new employees outlining how the company started, how much we have grown, why we're successful, where we're going, what we expect from employees, and what they should do if they have a problem. I introduce them to our concept of customer service and familiarize them with our corporate culture using anecdotes and examples.

I recently talked about indoctrination as part of a speech I gave to a group of entrepreneurs. Afterward someone in the audience said, "My company does the same thing, but we call it 'orientation.'" I don't consider what my company does "orientation." Orientation has no teeth and requires little from the people being oriented. When I think of orientation, I think of going off to college and getting a tour of the campus. Indoctrination, on the other hand, draws employees into your company and gets them to buy into your corporate culture from the get-go. One of the main points I try to convey is that we want happy customers. To do so, we need happy employees, or at least, "happy enough." I also emphasize that employees should talk to their supervisors if something bothers them. I then ask them to hold me accountable if they don't get the support they need. In addition, I ask new-hires to be my reality check by cluing me in if things aren't as I perceive them.

Lesson #65: Hook new hires from the start by indoctrinating them into your corporate culture.

Don't Play the Raise Game

What I Used to Think: You give employees a raise every year based on things like how much you can afford, how long they've been with your company, and their job performance.

Nobody Told Me: If you don't want to overpay employees, you need to develop a systematic method for determining pay scales. I give raises based on specific sets of criteria my managers and I developed for each position at my company. We weight the criteria according to what is most important in that position. Speed, for instance, may be weighted at 30 percent for a production worker and just 20 percent for a sales consultant. Quality control is very important in every position at my company, so it may be weighted at 40 percent for all employees.

Some other criteria we use include competency and leadership. We even give points to people who alert their supervisors to problems instead of just complaining to coworkers. One criterion we *don't* use is years of employment. That comes into play when we determine year-end bonuses.

When an employee has an annual review, we add up all of those percentages. Then we put that employee's total score against the base pay we have established. Let's say the base pay is $5.00, and the employee has been earning an hourly wage of $7.00. If the employee winds up with 50 percentage points on an annual review, he/she can earn $2.50 more than the base pay of $5.00, or $7.50. That's a fifty-cent raise. If the employee earns an hourly wage of $5.00, and earns 100 percentage points, he/she can earn 100 percent more than the base pay, or $10.00.

Linking raise reviews to specific criteria and establishing a base pay lets employees know exactly what you expect from them and what they can do to earn more money. It also helps ensure that your pay system truly is fair.

Lesson #66: Develop a pay scale if you want your pay system to be something more than a series of arbitrary decisions. Link the scale to job-specific criteria.

Don't Play the Bonus Game

What I Used to Think: You give hourly employees year-end bonuses based on their job performance.

Nobody Told Me: Year-end bonuses should not be one-minute raise reviews. Like raises, bonuses for hourly employees should be based on a formula everyone understands. I base them on the number of years someone has been employed with my company. A production employee who has worked at my company for a year receives $50. Employees receive an additional $50 each for every year they have worked for me. If they have been with me for twelve years, they each receive a $600 bonus.

Basing bonuses on years of employment makes it easier, in turn, to base raises on a specific set of criteria. No one says, "Gee, maybe we should give her a bigger raise. She's been here twelve years." You want to reward long-term employees monetarily but you don't want an overpaid workforce. It's very difficult to cut an overpaid employee's wages. Giving someone a $600 bonus, on the other hand, is a nice way to say thank-you. Using a simple formula also prevents employees from comparing bonuses and wondering why they got more or less than their coworkers.

I still give year-end bonuses. But many companies have successfully instituted profit sharing, in some cases, as an alternative to giving bonuses.

Lesson #67: Giving year-end bonuses doesn't have to be a gut-wrenching experience. It can be pleasant for everyone — including the boss.

Partying for the Bottom Line

What I Used to Think: You have a holiday party because that's what everyone does.

Nobody Told Me: A holiday party doesn't have to be a perfunctory event. It can boost employee morale. My company's holiday party has evolved from lunch ordered in for six employees sitting on boxes to a restaurant dinner for twenty employees and their guests to a banquet hall dinner for one hundred fifty employees and their guests, plus entertainment and a raffle.

Christmas is our busy season, so we hold our holiday party after New Year's Eve. The holiday party is a good way for me to thank everyone for their hard work. It also is a good opportunity for employees to get to know each other better. Even though my employees work in separate departments, they have to work as a team on every framing order. Giving people a chance to get to know each other personally reduces the level of friction that can arise among departments and increases cooperation. Working overtime keeps our employees away from home during the holiday season, so the holiday party also gives me an opportunity to say thanks to my employees' friends and family for their patience and understanding.

Some of my friends who work for law or accounting firms grumble about their office holiday parties, but most of the employees at my company look forward to this event. I run an hourly work force, composed, in part, of people who seldom attend formal events at fancy hotels or restaurants.

They get dressed to the nines and really kick up their heels. Everyone, for that matter, has a great time. Those employees who don't want to come know attendance is voluntary.

Lesson #68: Holiday parties are as much about business as they are about pleasure.

Giving Thanks ---- To Your Employees

What I Used to Think: My employees know I appreciate them.

Nobody Told Me: Your employees have no idea you appreciate them unless you tell them so. Express your gratitude to employees who have done a good job or put in long hours. I treat my employees to dinner, for instance, if they have to work late. It's one way for me to say thank-you. It saves them money and the trouble of having to find somewhere to buy dinner. Meals for employees are also tax deductible if they're served at the workplace.

On Saturdays I provide my sales consultants with lunch. It's not only a nice way to express my appreciation for their hard work on our busiest day, but it also is practical. Sales consultants have just half an hour for lunch on Saturdays because there's so much business. Providing lunch enables the sales consultants to eat and get back to work in a short period of time. It also saves them the hassle of having to bring their own lunches from home or running to the nearest fast-food joint.

Lesson #69: You can appreciate the hell out of your employees, but it makes no difference if they don't know it.

Defining Culture

What I Used to Think: New hires will figure out your company's corporate culture and make the necessary adjustments soon enough.

Nobody Told Me: Some employees never will understand or fit into your company's corporate culture. Keep the number of those people to a minimum by trying to define your company's corporate culture and clearly communicating it to prospective employees. I've identified three characteristics of my company that I always spell out to prospects.

The first is that we consider teamwork an individual responsibility. My employees work together as a team, but they have individual responsibilities. At some large companies, everyone works on everything, so it may be difficult to determine how hard each employee is working. There's nowhere to hide in my company. If you aren't doing your work, everyone knows it.

Another defining characteristic of my company is that we have a low tolerance for office politics. When employees are political, they primarily act in their own self-interest, not as a team member. We work very hard to keep office politics to a minimum. Anyone who attempts to get ahead here through political maneuvering not only fails but also alienates coworkers. If we make the mistake of hiring politicians, we ask them to change their behavior. (They usually don't or can't.) If they don't, we get rid of them.

The third defining characteristic of my company is that working here is an adventure. Adventure implies some risk or, at least, an element of the unknown. My company is a dynamic, growing entity, where there's a lot of opportunity and some risk. Management-level job descriptions need to be flexible here. Some people enjoy the challenges this kind of environment offers. Others find it intolerable.

I'm describing some key aspects of my company's corporate culture, but your company may be different than mine. You can save yourself and your employees a lot of grief by trying to define your company's corporate culture and clearly communicating it to prospective employees.

Lesson #70: Companies are not "one size fits all" when it comes to corporate culture.

Part IV – Customer Service:

Getting Beyond the Hype

Like Money in the Bank

What I Used to Think: Customer service is something extra you do to make customers happy.

Nobody Told Me: Providing great customer service and having a great product that's priced right are a powerful combination likely to result in explosive growth. I had very little money when I started my business. All I had was the desire to take good care of my customers, which I knew how to do because I had worked at my father's dime store when I was a kid. You could say I was weaned on customer service, though I didn't realize it until much later in my life.

I financed the growth of my business with customers who spread the word about my service and gave us their business again and again. Making customers happy is a cheap form of advertising. It takes money to hire the right employees and provide customer service training, but those costs are low compared to the cost of advertising. There are many things you can do for your customers that cost next to nothing. It just isn't that expensive to answer your phones quickly, greet people when they walk through the door, help customers to their cars now and then, exchange something for them, or provide them with a little extra information.

Another key to giving great customer service is your own attitude about customer service, and that really is a freebie. There's an old saying that when the fish rots, it rots from the head. If you place a high value on customer service, you will probably hire like-minded managers and put systems in place to help ensure the quality of your products and services.

That's how a customer service mentality permeates an entire organization and becomes part of its corporate culture.

Lesson #71: Your company's great customer service gives even your most fierce competitor's best ad campaign a run for the money.

Flow-Through Marketing

What I Used to Think: The key to growth is to constantly chase down new customers.

Nobody Told Me: It's OK to concentrate on bringing new customers through the front door so long as old customers aren't walking out the back door. One of the most effective ways to grow your business is to develop your existing customer base. It's cheaper to work your own customers for repeat business and referrals than to go after new customers. Studies show that the majority of customers stop doing business with you not because they have had a bad experience but because they're indifferent. You need to do whatever you can to make customers love doing business with your company. It's very difficult to grow most businesses without having a tremendous repeat customer base. Put as much energy into thrilling existing customers as you do into attracting new customers.

I've been through a few banks since I first started my business twenty years ago. I never was lured away by another bank. I left because I was dissatisfied with the service or the credit line a bank gave me. I rarely find out when the bulk of my customers stop doing business with my company. But when a customer—especially one with a commercial account— drops a bank, that bank knows.

"Wait a minute Mr. Goltz! Before you leave our bank, we'd like to talk to you. We don't want to lose your business and would like to see if there's anything we can do to convince you to stay. At the very least, we'd like to know what went wrong so we can prevent the same thing from happening to someone else."

How man times do you think a bank executive said that to me? Zero. Do you know why? Because those bank executives were too busy with marketing meetings. I call it *flow-through marketing*, and it's highly ineffective. If someone at one of those banks happened to notice they lost yet another customer, he/she probably rationalized, "We lost him, but our new advertising campaign will bring in plenty of new ones " Many companies count on losing customers, call it attrition, and forget about it. It's not good enough to anticipate losing a certain amount of business each year. You need to do whatever you can to prevent those losses or at least take the time to find out why your customers are leaving.

Lesson #72: Watching your back door is as important as watching your front door.

Anyone Seen a Study on Common Sense?

What I Used to Think: You should stay on top of those studies put out by those *really smart* people at think tanks, universities, and consulting firms.

Nobody Told Me: Few studies beat common sense in helping you run your business. I read a report that unhappy customers tell more people about their bad experiences than happy customers tell people about their good experiences. That's interesting, but I think businesspeople should make their customers happy because it's the right thing to do. It makes me wonder whether there are persons who, prior to reading this or that study, thought, "So what if I tee off a customer now and then?" I don't know. But I do know that nobody worth his/her salt needs a statistic to tell it pays to make your customers happy. It also is the right thing to do.

Of the many successful companies I've observed, they did well, not because of scientific studies, but because of their common sense. They saw something in the marketplace that they could do better. They pioneered new strategies or restructured old ones to outperform their competitors. They were proactive, based on their own observations and common sense.

Lesson #73: A little common sense goes a long way in business.

No One's Always Right, Not Even the Customer

What I Used to Think: The customer is always right.

Nobody Told Me: This cliché certainly does a good job of reminding us to always be respectful of our customers and to treat them well. But it falls short as a customer service training tool. This mantra actually frustrates your employees more than it helps them provide better customer service. Yes, it tells them that customers ultimately are the ones who pay their salaries, but I think there are better ways to communicate that message. We all know customers sometimes are wrong, sometimes make unreasonable demands, and sometimes behave shamefully. If you're telling employees the customer is always right, you're telling them to deny reality.

I tell my employees, instead, to *pretend* that the customer is always right. Then I explain why that's so important. I find that customers are right about 95 percent of the time. If employees think a customer is wrong, I encourage them to put themselves in the customer's shoes before they make a final judgment. Maybe 4.5 percent of the time, the customer *is* wrong, but it just makes no sense to argue. We're not here to win arguments. We're here to make money, and the way we do that is through repeat business and referrals.

I demonstrate how much money it costs to replace a customer through marketing and advertising. It's easy to show how much more cost-effective it is to spend $50 or $100 to resolve a customer problem than to risk losing that customer, whether right or wrong. A customer may be wrong and think

132

he's right or be wrong and know it. There's no way to tell. So it's easier to pretend the customer is right, take care of the problem, and let the customer feel good about the experience.

We're left now with what happens the remaining .5 percent of the time. That's when you know the customer is wrong, and resolving the problem will cost your business an exorbitant amount of money. These situations are best managed on an individual basis by you or a manager. You often can work out satisfactory deals with dissatisfied customers and avoid a lot of unpleasantness without losing your shirt.

Lesson #74: It's time to lose the "customer is always right" mantra.

There's No Margin for Error When You're Talking about Customer Service

What I Used to Think: If your company does more than 99 percent of everything right the first time, you have nothing to worry about.

Nobody Told Me: If my company does more than 99 percent of everything right the first time, most customers eventually will have a problem. Given the high number of variables in framing and the large role personal preference plays in customer satisfaction, I'm proud my customers accept more than 99 percent or our work. Nonetheless, that 1 percent concerns me. Just because customers are pleased with more than 99 percent of our work doesn't mean 99 percent of our customers are happy. Many customers not only give us repeat business, but also bring several framing jobs in at a time. Chances are, they eventually will have a problem with an order.

That's why it's crucial my employees know what to do should any customer problems arise. Training and empowerment are the keys to successful problem resolution. My sales consultants are trained to anticipate problems and execute their solutions with grace and ease.

Lesson #75: A customer problem is an opportunity to demonstrate just how good your company is.

Everyone's a Critic

What I Used to Think: Customers recognize that your company provides great service, or at least has good intentions.

Nobody Told Me: Customers in general, and new customers in particular, may pass judgment on your entire company based on one experience with one employee. If that experience happens to be a bad one, that customer may very well conclude that your entire company stinks. You can have phenomenal customer service, an outstanding product, and an excellent location. But if one employee on just one occasion provides poor service to a customer, that customer probably will indict the whole company. All it takes is one employee to tarnish your company's reputation with a customer. That employee can be anyone from a receptionist or delivery person to a sales consultant or manager.

If you call a cab company with 2,000 cabbies and get stuck in the back seat of one who's a jerk, you may not only conclude that the entire cab company is no good but also that all cabbies are jerks. That's human nature. We often make broad-based generalizations when we shouldn't. Well, your customers are human, too. That's why I tell my employees every single contact with a customer is critical.

Lesson #76: You're only as good as your worst employee.

Just Say No to "Yes"

What I Used to Think: "Yes" is the best answer your employees can give.

Nobody Told Me: "Yes" is an anemic answer. If you really are serious about customer service, you should know there are better answers than "yes."

Say you just moved to a new town. You own an exotic car. Say it's a Lotus. You need to have it repaired, so you call six auto repair shops. Where do you take it? To the place that answered "Yes" when you asked whether they know how to repair a Lotus? Or to the place that answered, "Absolutely, we specialize in imports, and the shop's owner drives a Lotus"?

Maybe you're just shopping for some clothes. You ask an employee to find a shirt in your size. Wouldn't you rather hear someone say, "Sure, I'd be happy to. I'll be back in just a moment" than "Yes"? If you want your employees to provide comfort, demonstrate credibility, or just show that they're eager to please, instructing them to say "yes" won't cut it. There always is a better answer than just "yes."

Lesson #77: The answer "yes" is about as exciting as kissing your sister.

Nice SAVE

What I Used to Think: If you want to provide great customer service, just tell employees that no customer should ever be left unhappy.

Nobody Told Me: Even the most outgoing, eager-to-please employees need customer service training. I not only provide employees with customer service training but use the acronym *SAVE* to help them manage customer problems. No matter how hard you try to give outstanding customer service, if you have more than a handful of employees and do a lot of business, a customer eventually will be unhappy. *SAVE* helps my business hold on to customers whom we otherwise might lose. What does *SAVE* stand for?

Well, the *"S"* stands for *sympathize*. When a customer tells you about a problem, the first thing you should do is acknowledge it and sympathize. Just saying, "Yes, I see what you're talking about and understand why you're upset," can provide comfort to an unhappy customer. If the customer is very angry, it may diffuse the attack.

"A" stands for *act*. Sympathy only goes so far. At some point you have to do something to resolve the problem. At my company action means anything from contacting a manager to offering to redo a frame right away.

"V" stands for *vindicate*. We do the job right more than 99 percent of the time. When we do make a mistake, I want customers to know that it's an unusual occurrence. I had a suit tailored recently and noticed that the pants were too short when I tried them on. I asked the tailor, "Does this kind

of thing happen often?" He said, "Sure, all the time." Well, I found another tailor after hearing that. It's reassuring to customers if you honestly can tell them, "An inspector checks over each order before we give it to a customer. It's very unusual for them to miss something like this," or whatever you can say to indicate you ordinarily do the job right.

Lastly, *"E"* stands for *eat* something. You haven't redeemed yourself just because you haved solved the problem. Your customer didn't come to you to have a problem. How many times have you ordered out for chop suey and discovered when you got home that the rice, sweet-and-sour sauce, or something else was missing? It's a thirty-minute round-trip drive between your house and the restaurant. The last thing you want to do is get back in your car to pick up the missing item, but the meal won't taste as good without it. You're aggravated, so you call the restaurant to complain. Maybe they apologize and offer you a credit for the rice you never received. Well, that don't cut it. I'd like them to apologize and deliver the rice immediately. I'd like them to apologize and offer me a credit for half the bill. Better yet, I'd like them to make sure my order is complete before I pick it up. I don't want to just come out even because I've been inconvenienced.

You owe something to a customer when you fail to deliver as promised, not just because it's the smart thing to do but because it's the *right* thing to do. It costs you some money in the short run to eat something, but in the long run it saves you money. It costs much more to lose and replace a customer than it does to *SAVE* a customer.

Lesson #78: Companies that have great customer service have great customer service training.

The "Hi, How Are You?" School of Customer Service

What I Used to Think: Every company knows what great customer service is.

Nobody Told Me: Many businesses confuse being polite with providing good customer service. I went to one of the big sporting goods chains the other day and felt like I was at a high school reunion. You go to your high school reunion and only have time for the most superficial conversations because there are so many people you know and want to greet. At the sporting goods store, someone greeted me at the door. Then every time I turned a corner another salesperson said, "Hi, how are you? Hi, how are you?" Every once in a while you run into salespeople who say, "Hi, let me know if I can help you." That's great, except that when you ask for help, they're often at a loss. They don't know where anything is or have any more information about the products than you do.

To provide great customer service, your employees need to be knowledgeable, not just polite. I don't want to be greeted by every salesperson who works in the store. I want employees who can help me find what I need and who know something about what they're selling. The smiles and greetings are very nice, but they don't constitute customer service.

If you want to provide great customer service, you have to look beneath the surface to determine what that means at your company. Once you figure that out, you to have to provide employees with customer service training, implement a monitoring system to make sure it's being delivered, and hold employees responsible when they fail to give great service. If customer service were as easy as being polite, Nordstrom's, the legendary, Seattle-based department store known for customer service, wouldn't be considered a phenomenon. Anyone who's bought anything recently knows great customer service is the exception rather than the rule.

I make fun of the companies that have smiling employees greeting you at every turn. But these companies deserve more credit than those companies whose employees don't even try to be pleasant. I used to tell my employees to be happy around customers. Usually my employees just listened and nodded their heads, but once a sales consultant asked, incredulously, "We have to be happy?" She was right, of course, to question me. You can't reasonably expect anyone to be happy, but you can expect employees to act happy. Now I tell them, "If you can fool me, more power to you."

Lesson #79: There's a big difference between knowing customer service is important and delivering it.

Knowing When to Bring Out the Big Guns

What I Used to Think: Employees have to learn how to manage difficult customers.

Nobody Told Me: There are times when you or a manager may have to protect employees from abusive customers. There are some customers who will take advantage or even abuse your employees but treat you with all the respect in the world. I've seen customers lay into young sales consultants, make all kinds of demands, and then totally back off the minute a manager or I entered the picture. Some customers are disrespectful toward younger people. Others are contemptuous of members of the opposite sex. They may take their problems and frustrations out on your employees.

When you or a manager sees a situation like that unfolding, you owe it to your employees to step in and diffuse the tension. It's unfair and unwise to leave an employee out there dangling under those circumstances. By stepping in you can avert a scene in your place of business and demonstrate to your employees that you're behind them.

I'm not suggesting that you come to the rescue every time there's a customer problem. There are times when it's inappropriate for you or anyone else to intervene. I remember having dinner with my wife at a restaurant. She ordered a sandwich with lean meat, but when the waitress brought our food to the table, we both could see the sandwich contained more fat than meat. My wife immediately, but very calmly, pointed out the problem. The waitress insisted on bringing over the manager. The manager brought her a new sandwich, but it made us feel uncomfortable. We didn't want to talk to the manager. We just wanted another sandwich. There clearly was no need to involve the manager in that situation.

Lesson #80: There are appropriate times in business when you have to bring out the big guns.

Hold on to Your Soul

What I Used to Think: There's nothing you shouldn't do to appease an unhappy customer.

Nobody Told Me: There can be a fine line between giving excellent customer service and selling your soul. I consider it offensive when a customer swears or says something like, "That's the most ridiculous thing I've ever heard!" But I also understand that people lose their cool when they're upset. I tell my employees we may have to take some abuse if a customer gets upset because we screwed up an order. They're adults and either have learned or are learning how to let rude remarks slide.

I also tell them there's a limit to the degree of abuse I expect them to take. If a customer grabs an employee's arm, shouts obscenities, or makes a threat, for instance, he/she has gone too far. My employees know that if they feel frightened or threatened by a customer, a manager or I will extricate them from the situation.

Sometimes customers are abusive without ever raising their voices. I had a big account who thought nothing of canceling purchase orders after we were halfway done with them. We tried to resolve the problem, but to no avail. Moreover, they were arrogant about the situation. It was so aggravating, I considered dropping their business. I thought, "I'm not going to go broke if I lose this account. I won't have to lay off any employees. I'm willing to lose some money because the price of doing business with this customer isn't worth the aggravation." If losing the account had put me at risk of going under or having to make layoffs, maybe I would have reached a different conclusion. Business people have to make that decision on their own.

Another sticky customer service issue is where to draw the line on giving refunds for custom merchandise. I'm not talking about those instances when your company has screwed up. I'm talking about those times when you've done everything right and the customer still is unhappy. It's easy to say the customer is always right and to give a refund to any dissatisfied customer if you're selling ice cream. If you're selling high-ticket items, however, it's another story. What if you're in the heating, venting, and air conditioning business? You install a $3,000 air conditioner, and your customer says, "You know what? I don't like it. It makes a whooshing noise whenever the air comes on. I don't want it." Every company needs to determine where to draw that line.

Lesson #81: Don't kid yourself. Even companies that are famous for customer service have limits.

Hey, Thanks!

What I Used to Think: The only way to thank customers is to give them great products and service.

Nobody Told Me: Giving great products and service to customers is the best way to say thank-you for their business, but not the only way. Sometimes you want to do something extra to let your customers know how much you appreciate them. I thank my customers during the holiday season by sending a greeting card with a ticket they may redeem for a bottle of wine at our stores. Thousands of customers come in with their wine tickets. We also serve wine, cheese, and other snacks every Saturday between Thanksgiving and Christmas. Customers often tell us how much they appreciate the gesture.

I also try to do something special for those customers who give us a lot of business. It turns me off when I shop at stores with preferred customer programs. Some businesses confer the "preferred" designation on one group of customers, sending the rest of their customers a message that they don't matter.

There are more sincere ways to recognize your best customers. Rather than a phony preferred customer gig or giving special services, or discounts, I send a gift with a note expressing my appreciation. We recently gave a National Geographic book of photographs to our customers. They thought it was terrific. People come here to decorate their homes, so it was appropriate to give them a coffee table book filled with magnificent pictures.

Lesson #82: There are many innovative ways to say thank-you to customers.

Part V – Marketing:
What the Hell Is It?

The Three-Legged Stool

What I Used to Think: If your marketing efforts are successful, and you continually bring in more and more business, everything else will take care of itself.

Nobody Told Me: You can be super busy and go broke. Business is like a three-legged stool. It has a marketing leg, finance leg, and management leg. If one leg of your stool is much longer than the other two, you will fall on your butt. The same is true for business. If you enjoy and are good at marketing, that's likely to be the longest leg of your stool. Many entrepreneurs come out of the gate fast because they're talented salespeople. Many of those same entrepreneurs fail miserably because they never figure out how to run a business.

I came out of the gate flying because I provided high-quality framing, gave customers great service, and ran good print and radio advertisements. Referrals came in left and right, and my business was growing at an annual rate of 100 percent. My marketing leg was long, but my finance and management legs were short. The more the business grew, the more complicated my finances became. I had to turn my attention to finance, educating myself about credit lines, receivables, and cash flow, among other matters. My business eventually got big enough to support a controller.

Now that I've built up my strength in finance and management, I need to devote more energy to marketing. Once again, I'm chasing the short leg of the stool.

Lesson #83: What you don't know *can* kill you.

Jay Goltz

The Difference between Marketing and Selling ----
Lost Revenue

What I Used to Think: Marketing and selling basically are the same thing.

Nobody Told Me: The best marketing in the world doesn't mean a thing if you don't know how to sell. *Marketing* is figuring out who your customers and prospects are and how to get their business. *Selling* is what you do once you've established contact with customers or prospects.

I was at a seminar for entrepreneurs sponsored by one of the big copy machine companies. I happened to need a new copier and was very impressed by the sponsor's presentation. They had a row of machines lined up and numerous people demonstrating each machine's capabilities. I asked one of these people for help, but he said he was from the color division and suggested I come back later to meet with the salesperson from the black-and-white division. I came back and found the right guy, but he said he couldn't quote any prices and suggested I contact a local salesperson.

When I returned to Chicago, I called the local outfit. They sent a salesperson out to make a presentation. His presentation was mediocre at best. I never bought a copier from that company. I was in the mood to buy and had my charge card ready at the seminar, but they blew it.

I see this happen all the time. Companies sink small fortunes into elaborate trade show displays, gorgeous brochures, and mass mailings, then fail to follow up with a hot prospect. Sometimes they go as far as sending out some lame salesperson who doesn't know how to give a presentation or close a sale. These companies have the marketing down, but not the selling.

Some companies, on the other hand, are better at selling than marketing. It's an inefficient way to do business. It's time consuming to educate potential customers who never have heard of you or your company. You also can waste a lot of time going after the wrong customers if you fail to do your marketing homework and don't know who your best prospects are.

Lesson #84: Selling without marketing can be inefficient. Marketing without selling can be disastrous.

Slaying the Mediocrity Dragon

What I Used to Think: The competition is the enemy.

Nobody Told Me: The enemy is mediocrity. Instead of watching the competition, watch the receptionist who lets the phone ring too many times, the salesperson who's rude to a customer, the production worker whose workmanship is shoddy. That doesn't mean you should be oblivious to your competition. It only means business owners are better off spending their time figuring out how to improve their products and services than thinking about what the competition is doing.

Obviously you should be aware of what your competitors are doing and stay on top of things like their advertising, selection, and pricing. My point is, spend most of your time watching your own business rather than your competition's.

Lesson #85: Make the competition watch you.

Eeny, Meeny, Miney, Moe ---- Choosing Your Best Customer

What I Used to Think: You can be everything to everybody.

Nobody Told Me: You can die trying. The things you do to attract high-end customers are the same things that drive low-end customers away, and vice versa.

If you want to bring in upscale customers to a restaurant, you will have to sink money into attractive furnishings, an outstanding chef, an experienced wait staff, beautiful menus, and fine ingredients. Accordingly, you'll need to price meals higher than most low-end diners can afford.

If, on the other hand, you want to sell good, reasonably-priced food, you will have to cut back on amenities. That may turn off high-end diners, who are used to high-quality service and beautiful surroundings.

If you target upscale consumers, you may attract some middle-end consumers but no low-end consumers. There usually is some overlap. It's unlikely, however, that you will get all levels of consumers. You have two choices when it comes to pricing if you target high-end consumers by doing everything first class. You can try to keep your prices down so you can hold on to the low-end people. Or you can raise your prices to cover your costs and risk losing some low-end customers. If you do the former, you will be very busy but make very little money because of your expenses.

Lesson #86: Figure out who your best customers are and focus more energy on them.

Right Message, Wrong Medium

What I Used to Think: Television must be the best advertising medium because that's what the big companies use.

Nobody Told Me: You can waste a lot of money advertising in the wrong medium. There are many reasons why some products and services work well in one medium but not in another. Perfume companies, for instance, rarely advertise on the radio because they sell scents based on sex appeal. Sex appeal, more often than not, is communicated visually. Department stores, on the other hand, rely heavily on newspaper advertising because it allows them to display a lot of sale merchandise and list sale prices.

I considered television advertising a few years ago but concluded it would be a waste of money. Television's reach is too broad for my business. If I had twenty stores in metropolitan Chicago or were in the kind of business that attracts customers thirty miles away, a television ad might pay. I have three locations, and most of my customers live within ten miles of each store. It makes more sense for me to advertise in a medium targeted at people who live or work near my businesses.

Lesson #87: Spend a lot of time and energy finding out who your customers are and how to reach them.

Your Best Ad May be Your Address

What I Used to Think: If you want to keep your costs down, rent is a good place to start.

Nobody Told Me: Low rent probably has put more people out of business than has high rent. I've found that paying $2,000 more each month for rent in a high-traffic neighborhood brings in more business than spending $2,000 each month on advertising.

I'm not suggesting that everyone rush out and rent the most expensive space available. I am suggesting is that you consider location, in part, a marketing expense and budget accordingly. There are many things to think about when choosing a location, including how much space you need, foot traffic, and image.

If you need a gigantic space, the difference between locating in a low-rent district and a mid- to high-rent district could be cost-prohibitive regardless of the marketing benefits.

Foot traffic is critical for some retailers but negligible for others. If you sell a small number of very high-ticket items, you may not need a lot of traffic. You might be better off spending your money on highly targeted advertising than rent. Service businesses and manufacturers generally are less reliant on location than retailers. If you own an electric motor repair shop, most of your customers probably find out about you through the Yellow Pages. Foot traffic is irrelevant, though it may be beneficial to locate in an industrial district so you're close to your customer base.

A third consideration is image. A stockbroker needs to project an image of prosperity and benefits by having an office in a prestigious building or neighborhood. Someone selling prosthetic devices, on the other hand, has no need for a tony address.

Lesson #88: Rent is frequently as much a marketing expense as it is a cost for space.

What I Learned from Buying a Pair of Shoes

What I Used to Think: You learn what you need to know only from people in your industry.

Nobody Told Me: You can learn something, for example, from a shoemaker. You can adapt other people's great ideas to your own business, even if they're in another industry. I'm naturally curious and observe everything I can in life. I bought a pair of Allen Edmonds shoes several years ago and was impressed by the packaging. The Wisconsin-based company makes high-quality, hand-crafted shoes. The shoes I bought came in an attractive fabric bag with a drawstring. I immediately thought, "What a nice presentation! What a good shoe this is!" Followed by, "I really like these bags. Is there any way I could use them in my business?"

It occurred to me that we could present fillet samples to customers in similar bags. A *fillet* is a decorative piece of wood that goes around the inside of a frame. It's a deluxe framing option that may significantly increase the cost of a framing order. Our framing consultants had kept them bound with rubber bands under their framing stations.

I called Allen Edmonds to find out who made their bags, contacted that company, and ordered a roll-out bag specially designed for our fillet samples. Now we present the entire selection of fillets to customers by rolling a beautiful bag out on the counter. It helps our framing consultants keep the samples organized and looks great.

Lesson #89: You can get great ideas for your business by observing the most mundane things.

Shut Up and Listen

What I Used to Think: You're the expert on what your customers want.

Nobody Told Me: Your customers are the experts on what they want. I initially thought my business was growing because my prices are good, but I eventually realized that customers like doing business with my company because we provide a superior product. Granted, customers may be reluctant to tell you they like your prices, but they also are unlikely to extol the quality of your products for no reason. Customers often exclaimed, "Wow, this looks beautiful!" I didn't know what all the fuss was about. Then it occurred to me that other framers weren't doing as good of a job as we were. I took it for granted that everyone did a good job.

I expanded my delivery service after a customer told me how difficult it was to transport a large picture from our store to her home. We would have been happy to deliver it, but we didn't advertise our delivery service, and she didn't think to ask. Now I make sure everyone knows we deliver. As a result, roughly 20 percent of our customers use our delivery service.

Customers are your best source of information on what they want and need. Sometimes they will tell you straight-out what changes you should make. More often, they will just provide information from which you have to draw the right conclusions.

Lesson #90: Listening may be one of your most effective marketing strategies.

How About a Twelve-Step Program for Retailers Who Can't Resist Running Sales

What I Used to Think: It must be good business to run big sales because that's what most retailers do.

Nobody Told Me: Big sales can wreak havoc on your bottom line. You might generate some additional traffic, but your margins are likely to suffer. Sales can be a great marketing strategy for some businesses because they increase visibility and foot traffic and help move stale merchandise.

In the framing business, running sales presents some problems due to price integrity. Every day my sales consultants and I hear customers exclaim, "How could it cost $150 to frame a poster?" One of our greatest challenges is to educate customers about the costs that go into each framing job. I'm talking about custom framing, in which handmade materials may be used and each frame is put together by hand. It's a very labor-intensive process, from cutting the mat, the glass, and the frame, to assembling all the pieces. How would it look if a week after explaining to a customer why it cost $150 to frame a poster we said, in effect, "Just kidding. Every frame job is 30 percent off"?

Price may initially be the primary selling point for many people. But value, quality, service, selection, and location often are what bring customers back. I emphasize service in my advertising, because that's an important distinction for someone in my business. Unless you have some great cost advantage that allows you to undercut your competitors without cutting into your margins, you will pay for running big sales. Make sure you understand the costs involved in using big sales as a major marketing strategy.

Lesson #91: Running a lot of big sales may succeed only in making you really busy before you go broke.

Sales Nirvana

What I Used to Think: Trade shows are too big of an investment for small companies.

Nobody Told Me: Trade shows have revolutionized the business world in the twentieth century. Before trade shows, businesspeople had no other choice than to travel far and wide to find new customers. Trade shows, on the other hand, present you with thousands of customers who are looking for what you're selling. You may have to travel to another city or even another country to participate, but that's easier than traveling to twelve cities and dragging product samples and sales literature from one potential customer to another.

Trade shows aren't cheap, but you have to compare the cost of attending them with the cost of other sales and marketing vehicles. You could save money on displays and booth rentals if you don't attend trade shows, but you will probably still have to budget for sales trips and sales literature.

The real question to ask yourself before you sign up for a show is, "Are you prepared?" Do you have an attractive booth? Do you have brochures and sales materials? Do you have salespeople to follow up leads? There's a lot to know about trade shows, and it is worth it to take a class or read a book on them. The first trade show I did was a complete waste because I didn't know what I was doing. Once I learned the ropes, I found trade shows could generate valuable leads.

Lesson #92: Trade shows can open more doors than the Avon lady and the Fuller Brush man combined.

How Much Is Too Much to Spend on Advertising?

What I Used to Think: You should spend as much money on advertising as the business experts recommend.

Nobody Told Me: If you want your business to grow, you should spend as much money on advertising as you can without going broke. That may sound facetious, but there's a message here. Effective advertising pays for itself in the long run. It's a cash flow item in the short run and a profit item in the long run.

Most companies don't make money from their first contact with a customer. A customer may purchase something, but the profit from that purchase is unlikely to cover the cost of your advertising. If you do a good job, however, that customer may come back and bring in referrals. That's how advertising pays for itself in the long-run. If you spend $1,000 on an ad and it brings in $4,000 worth of business, your advertising costs are just 25 percent. If your cost of goods sold is 50 percent, you no longer are a business — you're a money machine—and I never have seen one.

If you're spending so much money on advertising that you have no cash left to pay your other bills, you'll go broke. If, on the other hand, you're spending less money on advertising than your cash flow can afford, you're not doing as much as you could to grow your company.

Companies may dedicate anywhere from 1 percent to 40 percent of their budgets to advertising. Your company's position in the marketplace is another important factor to consider when calculating the optimal percentage of your budget to spend on advertising. If the market allows you to raise your prices to finance your advertising, you may be able to devote a higher percentage of your budget to advertising than someone who has to keep prices low to be competitive.

Lesson #93: Those who say they have the magic formula for how much to spend on advertising probably also have a close personal relationship with the Easter Bunny.

A Good Advertising Agency is Hard to Find

What I Used to Think: If you hire an advertising agency, you'll get great ads.

Nobody Told Me: You get great ads, generally, when you have hundreds of thousands of dollars to spend on advertising. (Even then, there's no guarantee your ads won't flop with consumers.) The best advertising agencies make their money by charging big bucks to come up with the right creative message for *Fortune* 500 companies. Their prices are stiff because their clients are corporations that will pay just about anything to get an edge on their competition. These corporations spend huge amounts of money researching how to advertise their products and services. The agencies they use attract the best creative talent and bill their time out at big-company rates.

Small businesses have no choice but to use small advertising agencies. Their rates may be lower than the top agencies, but they still reflect the advertising industry's overall cost structure. Your $30,000 annual advertising budget still won't go very far. The agency won't be able to devote a lot of time trying to figure out what your company's message should be. Instead, they probably will come up with a clever play on words or something generic.

Some small agencies out there do good work, but you have to work hard to find them. You may have to go through three or four agencies before you hit pay dirt. Do your homework when selecting an advertising agency. Study each agency's portfolio and ask yourself whether any of the ads grab you. Talk to clients and ask if the agency welcomes their input. Once you've selected an agency, show proofs of their work to your customers and get their responses.

I've had good luck with a young agency that's hungry for business and has an affinity for my company. I respect their expertise as advertising professionals but still consider myself the final authority on my business. Considering how much money advertising costs, it makes sense to read a book or two on the subject. Advertising requires expertise, but any business owner should be able to grasp the basic concepts.

Lesson #94: Whether or not you have big bucks to spend on advertising, great ads are the products of advertising agencies that understand and are interested in your business.

The Ringside-Seats Authority

What I Used to Think: Advertising representatives are experts on advertising.

Nobody Told Me: Advertising representatives are salespeople who may or may not know anything about advertising. Advertising sales is a highly competitive field, and there's often a lot of turnover in advertising sales staffs. The ad rep who is calling on you today might have been selling cars, draperies, roofing, or extended warranties for appliances the previous week.

A sales rep used to try to sell me a coupon mailer. He told me that the hot dog stand down the street had really built his business using these coupons. I need to ask myself questions. If the hot dog customers were using coupons, would they have come in anyway? And, is selling hot dogs the same as selling picture framing? A sales rep may know advertising inside and out, but may fail to understand how your business works.

Be skeptical when advertisings rep tell you that a publication is right for your company or a that certain kind of ad would be most effective. Remember, they're not working for you, they're working for themselves and trying to make a sale. They may genuinely believe what they're telling you but not know what they're talking about. Don't assume they know what they're doing just because they *say* so. You'll see all combinations of know-how and salesmanship. A great sales rep may be selling an ad medium that's inappropriate for you. Or, a very poor salesperson may approach you with a product that would be great for you. Remember, you're buying the ad, not the salesperson.

Lesson #95: Advertising representatives have access to great tickets for sporting events. Don't mistake ad reps for advertising experts.

Great PR for about a Nickel

What I Used to Think: Public relations means getting media coverage.

Nobody Told Me: The real key to getting publicity is giving the media a unique angle, one that the public will find interesting. The first big article written about me called me, "the Henry Ford of framing." The article focused on changes in the industry. The reporter was drawn to the new and interesting twist.

Once you get coverage, you can get as much mileage out of a printed article or televised broadcast by reproducing it as you can from having it run in the first place. A major Chicago newspaper published an article about my company, and it brought in some new business. Reproducing it brought in even more business. I hung enlarged copies of the article up in my showrooms. It gave us credibility with new customers and reaffirmed what many longtime customers already thought.

I also included reprints in the marketing materials that my corporate sales consultants use for new business presentations. It's one thing to tell prospective clients that you're the biggest and the best, but it has much more impact when they hear it from a credible third party.

Lesson #96: You can get residuals from good PR.

Being Firm with Your PR Firm

What I Used to Think: If you hire a public relations firm, you will get publicity.

Nobody Told Me: I wish. You can waste tens of thousands of dollars on public relations firms. I've hired public relations firms, shelled out $800 per month for their services, and wound up without a shred of publicity in return. Sometimes you get nothing because they give it a good shot, but, hey, it just isn't your day, kid. Sometimes, however, you get nothing because the folks you hired are just incompetent or spend more time looking for new customers than working on your account.

I've hired six public relations firms. My experiences with five of them were failures. It's more difficult to determine if your public relations firm is incompetent than it is to determine if your advertising agency is incompetent. If an advertising agency gives you a bad ad, you can look at it, see it's no good, and take your business elsewhere. It may take months or even a year before a good public relations firm gets results, so it's difficult to tell initially whether your firm is doing a good job for you.

You have to be very cautious when selecting a public relations firm. Check references, make only short-term contracts, and continually monitor the firm's progress. You should be able to get an update every two to four weeks and be able to see progress. If you're not seeing any tangible results in a couple of months, I would starting asking more questions. Ask to meet the people who actually are working on your account, and ask them to keep records of all their phone calls and other activities on your behalf.

Lesson #97: Keep your public relations firm on a short leash.

Don't Let Your Yellow Pages Ad Reps Let Their Fingers Do the Walking through Your Marketing Budget

What I Used to Think: You can't go wrong with the Yellow Pages.

Nobody Told Me: The Yellow Pages help some businesses make fortunes but do nothing for others. Yellow Pages sales representatives are among the most aggressive sellers in the business. They come armed with facts and figures, but those statistics may not apply to your business.

If you're a plumber, car insurer, or electrician, the Yellow Pages probably is a great vehicle for you. That's true, in general, of businesses whose locations are relatively unimportant because they go to their customers or conduct most of their business over the telephone. Retail clothing stores and department stores, on the other hand, rarely have display advertisements in the Yellow Pages because consumers already know where they're located. Have you ever consulted the Yellow Pages because you needed to buy a new shirt?

Once you decide whether it makes sense for you to advertise in the Yellow Pages, you have to decide not only how big you want your ad, but also whether it should be in color or black and white. I determine size based largely on the size of my competitors' ads. Your little ad may be lost if all the other ads in your category are large. If your competitors' ads are small, on the other hand, you may not need a large ad. As far as color ads go, Yellow Pages representatives may tell you that they're more effective than black-and-white ads. I recently tried a color ad. It was very expensive and not worth the cost.

It's very important to rely on your own judgment, not that of a sales representative, when you purchase Yellow Pages advertising. One of my stores is in the middle of four different Yellow Pages regions. My sales rep advised me to buy listings in all four books. I did just that, writing off as a loss the 75 percent of each book that covered other areas. I eventually realized there are more cost-effective advertising venues and cut back on my Yellow Pages advertising for that store.

If you decide to go the display ad route, make sure you take the time and energy to develop a great Yellow Pages ad. Display ads are just too expensive to treat as listings. It also is important to track responses to your Yellow Pages ads. I track all of my marketing vehicles by asking my sales consultants to ask customers how they found out about us. Every time they enter an order on the computer, they are prompted to fill in that information. My marketing manager regularly reviews the responses so we can determine what advertising generates the most new business.

Lesson #98: The Yellow Pages can make a lot of money not only for advertisers but also for the people who print them. Beware.

Nothing to Sneeze At ---- 15 Percent Ad Commissions

What I Used to Think: Advertising media pay 15 percent commissions only to advertising agencies.

Nobody Told Me: If you do your own advertising, you should be able to negotiate a 15 percent discount with advertising media. Most advertising media don't care who gets the agency commission so long as they get your business. If they decline to negotiate a discount, you can always set up your own advertising agency. Call it ACME Advertising and bill your ads through it. It makes a lot of sense, especially if you run the same ads frequently. If you change your ad copy frequently, it might be more cost-effective to either hire an agency or let the in-house advertising staff of a newspaper, for instance, do the work *and* have the commission.

Lesson #99: You can recapture 15 percent of your advertising expenses.

Being Scrappy

What I Used to Think: There are no bargains in advertising.

Nobody Told Me: Remnant space is as close to a bargain as you're likely to find in advertising. *Remnant space* is what newspapers call space left over after they've laid out the pages. Many newspapers discount remnant space by as much as 50 percent. You provide the newspaper with, say, a half-page ad. They run it when they happen to have a spare half page. It makes their job easier because there always is a paid, albeit discounted, advertisement they can use as filler. The disadvantage to you is that it may not run where and when you want it. Remnant space, however, is a good way to get more bang for your buck if you can afford the unpredictability.

Lesson #100: Remnant space is one of the few bargains in advertising. Take advantage of it.

Down and Dirty Advertising

What I Used to Think: Good advertising costs big money.

Nobody Told Me: There are guerrilla warfare tactics in advertising that don't cost a lot of money. The company vehicle, for instance, is a cheap way to advertise your company every day of the week. My delivery vans are painted with pictures of smiling people having art framed, and, of course, my company's logo. People see the vans up close all over the city. It costs nothing but the price of the paint job. If you wanted a billboard ad, you would have to pay an advertising agency to design the ad and then pay the billboard company for the space.

If you're a wholesaler, it may not do as much good to advertise on your company vehicles. But you might consider some other avenues to get your name in front of customers and prospects. Maybe you have your company's name printed on packing materials. Maybe your drivers wear uniforms with your company name. Maybe you include a flyer with your monthly statements. Almost any blank space is a cost-effective advertising opportunity.

Lesson #101: You can get more mileage out of a clever idea than an expensive advertising campaign.

Not-So Subtle Reminders

What I Used to Think: Ad specialties not only are a waste of money but also are a luxury only big companies can afford.

Nobody Told Me: Ad specialties frequently bring in more than enough business to pay for themselves. A guy selling boxes came to see me about fifteen years ago, but I couldn't give him much encouragement because I was happy with my box supplier. He left a pocket knife with his name on it, which I held on to because it often came in handy. When my vendor messed up an order several years later, I decided it was time for change. I just pulled out that little knife from my desk drawer, called the guy who gave it to me, and he became one of my company's vendors. I never would have remembered his name or known how to reach him if not for that knife. There have been dozens of times when a few months after turning away a salesperson, I wound up needing the product or service after all. But I had no idea how to find that salesperson.

If you give letter openers to a hundred people and get business from less than 1 percent of them, you most likely have covered your costs. Ad specialties with your name and telephone number not only help people find you when they need you but also keep your name in front of the public.

Use your judgment when deciding what types of ad specialties to distribute. Keep in mind that they don't have to be expensive. I give out pencils. They're cheap, people love them, and they're nostalgic.

Lesson #102: You can find your way into a lot of drawers with ad specialties.

You Can Make a First Impression Only Once

What I Used to Think: Customers don't care what your showroom or employees look like so long as you do good work.

Nobody Told Me: What your mother told you about first impressions is true. You may not notice anymore what your workplace looks like, but customers will notice everything. If you have a messy bathroom, torn carpet, or sloppily dressed employees, that will register on some level with your customers.

I remember driving behind a dirty white bakery truck and wondering whether the bakery was as dirty as the truck. Perception is reality. You may own the most competent business, but if your workplace is a mess, people may assume you do sloppy work.

The same is true if you have a salesperson who looks as if he/she just rolled out of bed, fails to make eye contact with customers, or just doesn't project a professional image. I decided to establish a dress code for my employees after years of hoping that they would understand the phrase "appropriate attire." The problem is, they do understand, they just have a different opinion about what is appropriate. In some cases I had to be very specific. For example, our salespeople cannot wear blue jeans, sleeveless shirts or printed T-shirts. The key here is telling them *before* they take the job.

Lesson #103: In business, first impressions are formed every day.

A Sincere Thank-You vs. A Tin of Caramel Corn

What I Used to Think: If you're in business, you have to send holiday gifts.

Nobody Told Me: There are other ways to say thank-you than sending a gift. Sometimes a handwritten note that reads, "thank you for your business" is worth more than the most expensive box of designer chocolates.

Holiday gift giving has become perfunctory for businesses. I'm afraid to come into work around the holidays because every day another vendor or business associate sends a tin of caramel corn, box of cookies, ham, or some other food item that's only going to make me fat. I'm serious when I say I would rather not have these temptations streaming into my office for weeks on end.

I would much rather receive a handwritten note that says, "Dear Jay, Thank you for your business. I really cherish our ten-year relationship and look forward to working together for another ten years. We had a great year with the help of great customers like you. Best wishes for a prosperous New Year." Even a sincere phone call from a vendor leaves a more favorable impression than any of the dozens of holiday gifts, edible and non-edible, I receive each year. If you receive lots of gifts you may even cease to notice them after a while.

Someone recently sent me a box of cigars and I don't even smoke! If I were a former smoker, I might have been offended. I'm not suggesting that you should never send holiday gifts. I just think you first have to give some thought to what you send.

Lesson #104: Business is about relationships and people, not caramel corn.

Part VI – Finance:

Paper Profits but No Money for Lunch

Going with the Cash Flow

What I Used to Think: Companies go under because they're not making any money.

Nobody Told Me: You can make money hand over fist on paper and still become insolvent because you have too little cash flow. Success takes years, but failure takes just ninety days. The biggest deal of your life can put you under if your don't have enough cash flow to buy the materials you need, pay for additional labor, and wait for the receivable. If you can't risk being stiffed, your business could go broke. Growing companies are especially susceptible to cash flow problems for these reasons.

Companies go under because they no longer can pay their bills. Some companies grow so quickly they have to plow all of their profits back into the business and eventually become insolvent in spite of their "success." There are numerous ways to slow down your company's growth if you're unable to support it financially and don't want to try to get additional funding. You can stop hiring sales representatives, raise your prices, stop opening new locations, and/or cut back on your advertising. It often is too late, however, by the time business owners realize that they have to do something about their cash flow problems. Businesses can go from being profitable to broke in what seems like the blink of an eye.

On the other hand, companies that show little, if any, profit but have good cash flow can stay in business for years or even decades. I know of a warehouse club that never turned a profit but had great cash flow because they turned their inventory so quickly. They could take delivery of a load of soft drinks on Friday and sell all of it over the weekend. They had credit with their supplier, so they could wait thirty days before paying the invoice. Say the warehouse club purchased the soft drinks for $10,000 and sold them at a 20 percent markup, or $12,000. They had twenty-seven days before they had to pay for the soft drinks, creating positive cash flow to the tune of $12,000.

You may be wondering how this company could have made $2,000 on that one transaction and not be profitable." That's easy. Margin doesn't equal profit. Maybe 99 percent or even 100 percent of that $2,000 went toward expenses like payroll, rent, and health insurance.

Companies that operate this way eventually do go belly-up. But they can survive for years off the credit everyone extends, from their vendors to the electric company. One reason they eventually fail is weak financial control. They discover, for instance, that their payables were understated, inventory was overstated, or major receivables are uncollectible.

While it may be better to have great cash flow and no profits than to have great profits and no cash flow, a healthy business needs both cash flow and profitability. You have to keep a very close eye on your cash flow, and that means making projections, budgeting carefully, and making sure you can pay your bills in a timely fashion. Running out of cash may be one of the few unpardonable sins in the business world.

Lesson #105: Profit doesn't mean a thing if you can't pay your bills.

Having the Courage of Your Pricing Convictions

What I Used to Think: Price your products at the same level or lower than your competition.

Nobody Told Me: The business graveyard is overflowing with companies that went broke despite having the best prices in town and the highest customer volume. Just look at all of the electronic and drug store chains that have gone under in recent years. Your company can make the greatest products, give outstanding customer service, and still fail to turn a profit if you have priced your products incorrectly.

If your prices are too high, you may lose out on some business. If your prices are too low, you may be very busy but probably won't make enough money to offset your expenses. There are many factors that determine whether your company will turn a profit. Pricing is at the top of the list.

You may have your products priced right but give so many discounts that you wind up with the same problem as the guy whose products are priced too low. You may think you charge $100 for your widget, but you cut so many deals with so many customers that the average price of your widget really is $90. If you cut a deal with everyone who complains about your prices, you will go broke.

It takes courage to charge the appropriate price by limiting customers discounts. You risk losing some business, but that's better than losing your entire business. The second you begin matching the competition's prices, you no longer are in control of your business—your competitors are. I can list ten frame shops that discounted all over the place and no longer are in business. I can list just as many frame shops that have resisted the discounting frenzy, provided good service and a good product, and still are around to compete with me for business.

Lesson #106: Pricing is critical. Discounting can be a critical mistake.

Don't Give it Away

What I Used to Think: Any order is a good order.

Nobody Told Me: You're better off without some orders. If the only way you can get an order is to give a customer or prospective customer a better price than you can afford, that order probably isn't worth getting. You're in business not to get orders but to make money. It's very tempting when you're hungry and want to grow your business to go after any order you can get. Most of your competitors probably have about the same overhead as you have. It's unlikely that any of them regularly can beat your prices by much and still pay their bills.

It's tough to turn down business, especially from longtime customers, but sometimes you must. Typically, someone who has been a good customer for years says, "Your prices just aren't good enough anymore. If you can't do better for me, I'm going to give my business to someone else." So what do business owners do? Typically, they panic. Then they rationalize, "We'll give him the prices he wants. Our overhead already is covered. If we can hold onto his business by meeting the competition's prices, we'll make it up with incremental business." That may work for a handful of customers, but there always are more customers who want you to lower your prices for them.

I remember a long-time customer who received a competitive bid for 20 percent less than our price. I couldn't do any better than what I already was doing for him, so I had to let go of his business. The company this customer left us for screwed up his very first order. He came back to my company within a week. Had I met the competitor's price or even come down 10 percent, I would have been stuck for the rest of my days giving this guy a price I couldn't afford. I also have learned that if you provide excellent service and an excellent product, some of the customers who say they're going to leave don't.

Lesson #107: It takes courage to say no to an order. But if you want to make money, you will.

Growth Spurts

What I Used to Think: You want to grow your business as fast as you possibly can.

Nobody Told Me: When I first heard the term *controlled growth*, I thought, "Only a wimp would want controlled growth. I want to grow uncontrollably. I want to get on that horse and make it run like hell." I struggled with fast growth. As a result, I learned that controlled growth means being in control, which is a good thing.

There's a mathematical formula to determine how much you can grow and remain self-funded. To do that calculation, you first have to figure out how much money you need to invest in your business to generate a sales dollar. As your business grows, you will need more money to finance your inventory, receivables, office furniture, space, work in progress, and many other incidentals. After you estimate your investment needs, you can figure out how much money you will need in profit, after taxes, to support your growth. This is a process that is well worth the effort, and your accountant should be able to help you work through the "what-if" scenarios. If he/she can't, you have the wrong accountant.

If you can increase your profit by raising your prices, you can get away with faster growth. If you can't raise your prices, however, you may have to borrow money to finance the additional growth. That begins a cycle of borrowing you have to monitor very closely. Taking in equity money from other sources is another option, but that, too, has its disadvantages.

Lesson #108: If you aren't practicing controlled growth, you're out of control.

Locking Up the Cash

What I Used to Think: Your employees won't steal from you if you pay them decent wages and treat them well.

Nobody Told Me: Nothing could be further from the truth. Someone eventually will steal from you if you let it happen. When I first opened my business, I never locked the cash drawer. I was just twenty-three years old and didn't want my employees to think I didn't trust them. Besides, there were only about a dozen people working for me then. When money started disappearing from the cash drawer, I had to wonder which employee was the culprit. When you leave cash lying around, you not only risk turning a basically honest person into a thief because of the temptation but also turn all your employees into suspects.

Keeping cash under lock and key is only the most obvious financial control. You also have to watch your checkbook. Not only should you limit the number of people who can sign checks but also lock up your checkbook. It's not difficult for someone to forge your signature. Banks miss forgeries all the time.

Some other controls that have reduced theft at my company include holding employees accountable for every tool we give to them, monitoring gas usage, and requiring gas receipts for company cars.

Lesson #109: If you don't have financial controls, it's not a question of whether people will steal from you, but when.

Risky Business

What I Used to Think: Spend it and worry later. That's the American way.

Nobody Told Me: People talk about "going for broke" as if it's something noble. If you want to stay in business, you may not want to live by those words. If you want your business to grow, however, it may be appropriate to take calculated risks with your money.

Whether or not your business is growing, it's prudent to have safety nets. Most businesses have down cycles due to the weather, the overall economy, a competitor's advertising campaign, a fire, flood, or something else. Safety nets help prevent a business slowdown from putting you out of business. Safety nets include discounting your bills so you have room to slow down your payments without being penalized, having a bank credit line, and even holding unused charge cards with substantial credit limits.

I started my business with very little money. It grew very quickly, so I always was chasing money. I needed cash to finance my receivables and inventory. I gradually got more trade credit and a larger credit line at my bank, but there were times when even that isn't enough. It took me about fourteen years from the time I started my business to achieve a healthy debt-equity ratio and credit to spare. Now my payables are down, and I discount most of my invoices.

A friend recently told me that I live below my means. Well, he's right, and it feels good. I would rather live below my means than above my means. I'm able to think more clearly now about my business. I look forward to coming into the office every morning. I know if I make a mistake, it won't bury me or my business.

Lesson #110: Going for broke sounds exciting until you actually go broke.

Budgets Are Sexy

What I Used to Think: If you know how to make money, you can dispense with budgets.

Nobody Told Me: Running a lemonade stand is different than running Minute Maid. Budgets are critical to a company's success. Operating without a budget is like baking a cake by mixing up a lot of different ingredients, putting the batter in a cake pan, and hoping it tastes good when you take it out of the oven. I no longer just hope to make money at the end of the year, I *plan* to make money by careful budgeting. Unless you have a budget, it's difficult to monitor how you're doing and make the necessary adjustments.

I used to find out whether I made money by taking inventory at the end of the year. By then, of course, it was too late to change anything. Now I constantly monitor every dime that comes in and goes out of my company. I look at my overhead in relation to my sales, for instance, so I can adjust my markups if need be. I used to think more sales would fix everything. That's one of the biggest fallacies in the business world. More sales sometimes just mean more costs and do nothing for your bottom line.

Lesson #111: Careful budgeting may not sound sexy, but making money is.

What an Employee Really Costs

What I Used to Think: If you pay employees $6.00 an hour, you're really paying them about $7.00 an hour, or 15 percent more than their hourly wage, when you take into account direct expenses like social security and unemployment.

Nobody Told Me: Social security, unemployment insurance, workmen's compensation, and other related expenses are just the tip of the iceberg. Add indirect expenses like health insurance and the expense of just having an employee on the books, and you get closer to what an employee really costs. I estimate employees wind up costing your company 25 percent more than what you pay them. That means if you pay an employee $6.00 an hour, that employee really costs your company $7.50 an hour.

If that doesn't sound so bad, wait just a minute. I haven't even gotten into how much an hour's worth of labor really costs. If you factor in training, the learning curve, vacation time, holidays, sick days, breaks, time spent coming and going, you're lucky to get 85 percent yield out of every hour of labor. That means if you pay an employee $6.00 an hour, that employee really costs your company about $8.80 an hour ($7.50 divided by .85). In other words, an hour of labor probably costs between 50 percent and 100 percent more than your employee's hourly wage. If it takes an hour to frame a picture, my labor costs are more like $12.00 than $9.00 an hour.

You need to know what your labor really costs so you can price your goods or services accordingly. I had to determine the average cost of labor at my company and figure out whether it increased more or less than inflation. That meant looking at the average output of my employees. I regularly monitor how much labor goes into every product. You can't get an accurate measurement by observing one employee working on one product. It may take only one hour when you stand over the employee's shoulder, but fifteen minutes longer under ordinary circumstances.

Lesson #112: If you want cheap labor, go to China.

Jay Goltz

Finding the Bank of Your Dreams

What I Used to Think: You wow a bank with your brilliant business plan, and the bank loans money to you. That's their job.

Nobody Told Me: Banks are more interested in your collateral than in your hopes, plans, and dreams. Some banks, usually large ones, will accept some risk. Unfortunately, I've felt dissatisfied with and left numerous banks since I started my business twenty years ago.

My most recent experience with the banking industry, however, really opened my eyes. I found myself, once again, searching for the right bank. I shopped my financial statements around to six financial institutions. Most of my collateral is in inventory, so I was ready to meet with some resistance. Banks dislike lending money against inventory because the borrower might sell it off or it may be difficult to liquidate should the borrower default on a loan. Three of the banks I approached treated me as if I had leprosy, while the other three were killing each other for my business. They were competing to cut me the best deal and called me every week.

I soon realized the common denominator was size. The banks that were avoiding me were small. They didn't even have liquidation departments. They gave out so few loans that bad loans weren't an issue for them. The other three banks were major players in the market. They had full-blown workout and liquidation departments because they were aggressive players in the business loan market. They accepted the risk of loaning money to small businesses. After talking to

196

some other business owners, I realized that these three banks probably controlled 50 percent of the small business loans in metropolitan Chicago.

Many banks are little more than currency exchanges, second mortgage and car loan companies, or whatever else they can be without taking any risks. I could have spared myself a lot of anxiety and heartache if I had talked to other business owners or had just paid closer attention to which banks were targeting small business owners.

Lesson #113: Approaching the right banks is half the battle of borrowing money.

Investors, Schmestors

What I Used to Think: You can grow your business painlessly if you just find one solid investor.

Nobody Told Me: Losing someone else's money may be worse than losing your own. Investors can help you finance and grow your business, but having their money can be a tremendous burden. I learned early on from personal experience that I would rather grow my business more slowly than take on the responsibility of someone else's money. I opened a second framing showroom and enlisted an investor. Business initially was slower than I anticipated, and my partner began worrying. I wound up buying him out, which was best for both of us.

Many business owners have made fortunes by using investor money. They may be able to manage the pressures of taking and possibly losing other people's money better than the average person. Some people have no choice but to use investor's money to finance or grow a business. I've been able to grow my business without investors, albeit less quickly. I concluded a long time ago that growing my company isn't worth the burden of someone else's money. There's no doubt, though, that if you want to grow your company very quickly, you'll need someone else's money. if you do accept an investor's I suggest you find one who can also give you good business advice. The advice could be as valuable as the money.

Lesson #114: Just because your partner is silent doesn't mean you don't know they're there.

The Accountant Myth

What I Used to Think: Accountants know a lot more than you do about business.

Nobody Told Me: Many accountants are nothing more than tax preparers. Even the best accountant probably can't run your company. I used to think accountants knew everything about business from working so closely with so many companies. Just because you watch football games every Sunday, however, doesn't mean you can be a quarterback. Accountants, by the same token, can't tell you how to make money just because they look at financial statements every day. You have to figure out how to do that yourself. Good accounting never has made a business, but poor accounting has ruined a lot of them.

Your accountant is like a navigator on a ship. The accountant's job is to keep you appraised of things like your longitude and latitude. You may be doing a phenomenal job of steering the ship, getting through storms and narrow passages. But if you're going in the wrong direction, it doesn't matter. You're the one who has to pay the price if your accountant miscalculates your inventory or fails to tell you that you're growing too fast or your budget is unrealistic. You can't just leave financial matters in your accountant's hands and assume everything will be OK.

You have to hire an experienced accountant and ask that person to play a supporting role in running your company. When you're interviewing prospective accountants, ask them what they think are critical areas to watch. If they start talking about trust funds and tax planning, they may not understand growing businesses. Those things are important, but only after you've addressed issues like cash flow, inventory, and budgeting.

Lesson #115: Accountants aren't gods in gray suits. They aren't even minor deities, but they do play a vital supporting role in running your business.

There Is Such a Thing as Free Money

What I Used to Think: A 2 percent discount for paying a bill in 10 or 20 days isn't worth the hassle.

Nobody Told Me: You're better off borrowing money from the bank or a credit line than blowing discounts on your invoices. Say a vendor requires that all invoices be paid in 30 days but gives you a 2 percent discount on bills paid in 10 days. You don't take the discount and instead pay the vendor in 40 days. You have basically borrowed money from your vendor for 30 days. It was a loan lasting 30 days, or roughly one-twelfth of a year. That loan cost 2 percent of the invoice, which really means 24 percent. If every month you lose a 2 percent discount, that's like paying 24 percent interest over the course of a year.

Most people wouldn't take a loan out at a higher interest rate than most credit card companies charge, but that's exactly what you do when you forfeit discounts. If the discount is just 1 percent, it only costs you 12 percent. But that's still a lot to pay in interest, especially if you have the cash. If your vendors give you a 5 percent discount to pay your bills in 10 days and you fail to do so, you pay a huge amount of interest. That 5 percent is like an annual interest rate of 60 percent.

Let's say you buy $6,000 worth of materials each year ($500 each month) and never take the 5 percent discounts your suppliers provide. Instead you borrow $500, which you have to pay back in a year at 10 percent interest, or $50. That loan allows you to pay your monthly invoices from that vendor in 10 days. If you didn't take out the loan and lost the 5 percent discount, it would cost you $300 in lost discounts. You save $300 by discounting, but it costs you $50 in interest. You still are $250 ahead of the game. Even if the discount is only 2 percent, it will cost you $120 in discounts, which is $70 more than it would cost you to take out a $500 bank loan.

So unless you're seriously strapped for cash and have no other means of borrowing money, take cash discounts. It's cheaper even to borrow from your charge card than to forfeit a 2 percent discount, unless you string out your payables to 60 days or more. In that case, you effectively borrow money for 50 days, so the multiple is smaller. I don't recommend stretching out your payables unless you have no other choice. You not only make your vendors unhappy but also use up one of your safety nets.

Lesson #116: Discounting bills is a no-brainer way to make more money.

Negotiating Vendor Discounts Isn't Pretty

What I Used to Think: Suppliers give you their best price because they want your business.

Nobody Told Me: Many suppliers give you their best price only if they have no choice. The commission structure at some companies dictates that sales representatives make less money on discounted sales. The company offers you a discount as an incentive to buy more of their products, but reduces its sales representatives' commissions to offset some of the discount.

I was buying 5,000 feet of a particular picture-frame moulding each month, so my supplier offered me a 30 percent discount. A few months later another framer told me he got a 40 percent discount from the same company. I called my sales rep to find out what the story was, and he said he gave the other guy a better discount because he purchases 10,000 feet of moulding at a time. I said to my rep, "Don't you think I would've increased the size of my order had I known you would've given me a bigger discount?" My sales rep nonchalantly said, "OK, well, I'll give you 40 percent off from now on." You have to keep in mind that the difference between getting a 30 percent discount and a 40 percent discount isn't just 10 percent. It's closer to 14 percent because you're getting an additional 10 percent off the list price, not the discounted price. If you're making high-volume purchases, that adds up to a lot of money.

I learned from that experience to always ask vendors, "What's your best discount, and how much do I have to buy to get it?" If sales representatives earn lower commissions on discounted sales, they may not volunteer that information. Some companies and their sales representatives recognize that it's in their best interest to tell you what their best deal is up front, because it gives you an incentive to increase the volume of your purchases. Those companies provide you with information on volume discounts without any prompting. If your sales rep isn't forthcoming with that information, however, you had better ask.

Lesson #117: If you want your supplier's best discount, you have to work for it.

Giving Credit Where Credit Isn't Due

What I Used to Think: If you give people an open account, they will pay you, if not because they're honorable, because they're afraid of a bad credit reference.

Nobody Told Me: You can count on getting screwed if you give credit to your customers, but giving credit might still be the right business decision. Some credit customers will try to stiff you. They won't pay their bills until they know you're serious about collecting. Some people may never pay up no matter how many phone calls you or your collection agency maker. You may hire a lawyer and, if you're lucky, settle for half of what's coming to you. Or you can take a deadbeat customer to court and learn more about the legal system than you want to know.

There would be no problem if you could just decline to extend credit, but that's difficult to do if you sell to other businesses. They aren't structured to pay C.O.D. and can't do business with your company unless you provide them with an account. I've gotten my receivables under control by checking credit references thoroughly before giving anyone an account and by putting credit limits on every new account. You also have to build deadbeat credit customers into your cost structure. You have to pay someone, whether it's one of your own employees or a collection agency, to call customers who fail to pay their bills.

You may not have the stomach for collections, but be prepared. You occasionally may hear from delinquent customers who are unhappy about being asked to pay their bills.

Don't buckle under to complaints from these customers. You're entitled to ask them for your money.

Lesson #118: If you give credit, you have to manage your receivables.

Run, Don't Walk, to the Bank

What I Used to Think: There's not much you can do about cash flow but send out statements once a month and hope the money comes in sooner rather than later.

Nobody Told Me: There *are* a few things you can do to improve your cash flow. You can get your receivables more quickly by sending out statements twice monthly instead of once a month. You also can immediately deposit big checks from customers into your bank account. If you get a lot of checks in the mail, you can set up a lock box at the bank. The bank will deposit them immediately. You lose interest every day a check sits in someone's desk drawer. Additionally, if a customer tells you that they're about to mail a check, ask for overnight delivery or send one of your employees over to pick it up.

You also may want to consider trying to get more customers to pay up front for products and services. If you currently take deposits, maybe you could offer customers an incentive to paying for everything up front, or just request the total amount instead of half. It never hurts to offer customers that option. Some people prefer digging through their wallets just once.

Lesson #119: You may not have to call a plumber to make your cash flow.

Beware of Leasing

What I Used to Think: Like the articles on leasing say, you should lease what goes down in value and buy what goes up in value.

Nobody Told Me: Most of those articles are written by leasing agents who have a vested interest in telling business owners to lease what goes down in value. Leasing is an easy but expensive way to borrow money.

Nothing you will buy or lease for your business is likely to increase in value. Will you ever buy a desk and sell it five years later for more than the purchase price? No one will ever say to you, "That's a mighty good-looking desk. The market's up on those desks. You paid $200. I'll give you $300." You will be lucky to get $50.

So when you talk about the advantages and disadvantages of leasing equipment, you really are talking about things that depreciate in value. Say you need a computer system but have no money. It costs $10,000, so if you want to buy it you have to borrow money. If you borrow money from the bank, it costs $12,000 with interest. That may seem like a lot of money, but you'll pay even more money if you lease it.

If you are basically purchasing something through a lease, there aren't many tax advantages to leasing, either. If the lease arrangement doesn't meet the criteria of an operating lease, the IRS considers it a capitalized lease. That means you can't write it off as an expense over the term of the lease. You can, however, write off the depreciation.

So why would anyone lease anything? Cars are an exception because they have good resale value, and many manufacturers offer attractive deals just to get their cars on the street. But I'm talking about leasing things with little or no resale value. Well, there are a couple of good reasons. Having a limited borrowing base is one of them. You may need something but have limited access to borrowed funds. Say your credit line at the bank is $50,000, and you have no more assets to pledge. You may have to reserve your credit line for things like inventory and receivables that can't be leased.

Leasing basically enables you to increase your borrowing power. A lease is like a high interest loan. You often are required to make two payments up front, which obscures the amount of interest you're paying. Up front payments reduce the amount of the loan but increase the actual amount of interest. So leasing is more costly than borrowing from a bank. But if you have no other options, it can help you maintain good cash flow.

You may want to consider leasing if you need to borrow money for something else. When banks determine whether to grant you a loan, one thing they look at is your debt compared to your equity, or your debt-equity ratio. Say you borrow $20,000 from the bank to buy a car. That car shows up as an asset but but has no effect on your equity. The $20,000 loan, on the other hand, shows up as liability, which means you have increased your debt-equity ratio. If you lease the car, it's a true operating lease and won't show up as a debt on your books. That's called *off-balance-sheet financing,* and it can be highly advantageous if you're in a critical cash situation.

Lesson #120: Look before you lease.

The Plastic "Option"

What I Used to Think: Charge cards are not an option. The interest is just astronomical.

Nobody Told Me: Charge cards can be a godsend even at interest rates of 18 percent. Charge cards saved my butt for many years. They're not the ideal way to grow a business, but if you have no other choice, they're a viable alternative. If you have little or no collateral, it's difficult to get a bank loan. Charge cards provide you with unsecured credit (credit without collateral). Charge card companies charge high interest rates because extending credit without collateral is very risky. It's almost a taboo among business owners to even talk about relying on credit cards. The truth is, many small businesses have no other choice. They use them as a last resort and, ideally, get out from under their debt.

When I was growing my business, credit card companies were handing out charge cards left and right. Whether or not I was using my cards, just having them gave me peace of mind. I didn't enjoy having to borrow money from credit card companies, but it was child's play compared to worrying about bankrupting my business. I recommend every business owner have a few charge cards so long as you have enough discipline to use them only as a last resort.

Lesson #121: When you have no other options, paying 18 percent interest is a pretty good deal.

Part VII – Administration:

The Little Things that Can Kill You

Don't Wait for the Government to Cut Your Taxes

What I Used to Think: There's nothing you can do about unemployment taxes but pay them and complain.

Nobody Told Me: If you hire and manage intelligently, you may be able to cut your unemployment tax rate in half. I used to hire stupidly, fire stupidly, and pay the highest unemployment tax rate in Illinois. Unemployment rates, rules, and regulations vary by state. New businesses in Illinois initially pay a flat rate, which goes up or down in subsequent quarters based on how much you pay out in wages and how much former employees collect in claims. I've been able to get my unemployment tax rate down five percentage points over many years. You pay out on just the first $8,000, which means each year I save $400 per employee.

I contribute the decline to three factors, the first and most important of which is that I've learned to exercise tremendous caution in hiring.

Second, I sit down with my managers and review new hires after 28 days. In Illinois you have no unemployment obligations for employees who are with your company fewer than 30 days. If after 28 days we're not reasonably confident an employee is working out, we let the person go. I tell all new hires up front that we're employing them on a 29-day trial basis.

Third, we keep detailed employee records. If we have to get rid of an employee for just cause, we have documentation to support us.

At the very least, you should pick up some literature from your state and attend a state-sponsored or independent workshop on what you can do to reduce your unemployment rate. You also may want to consider hiring a company that fights unemployment claims. Whatever you do, don't just write your unemployment rate off as a cost of doing business.

Lesson #122: Keeping your unemployment rate in line is one more way to stay off the unemployment line.

Taking a Calculated Health Risk

What I Used to Think: Health insurance costs are exorbitant. You just have to pay the going rate.

Nobody Told Me: You can save a bundle by partially self-funding your health insurance. Being partially self-funded in my case means that I have a $5,000 deductible on employee health insurance claims but pay a low premium. If someone is hospitalized, I'm responsible for up to $5,000 of their expenses. That may sound like a lot of money, but I save more money by paying a low premium than I spend on deductibles. There's a stop-loss of $25,000 on my plan, so the risk is limited.

Your insurance company expects to make a profit on every dollar it risks on your business. So the more risk you absorb, the lower your premiums. Some large companies are totally self-funded for that reason. It's difficult for small companies to absorb that much risk, but you can save a lot of money by partially self-funding or employing some other alternative.

Lesson #123: The high cost of health insurance is enough to make you sick. There's no remedy, but partial self-funding helps.

The Squeaky Wheel Gets the Lower Workmen's Comp Rate

What I Used to Think: You have no control over your workmen's compensation rate.

Nobody Told Me: You may be able to lower your workmen's compensation rate by double-checking employee job classifications. The government classifies your employees according to what kind of work they do. The workmen's compensation rate varies with each classification.

I contested the classification the government assigned to the employees in my mat-cutting and fitting departments. They were lumped in with the glass and frame cutters even though they don't work with saws or anything else that might cause serious injury. I proved they should be reclassified into a category for which the workmen's compensation rate is several percentage points lower.

Lesson #124: Workmen's compensation is too expensive to leave to the Feds. Make sure your employees are correctly classified.

Gas, Water, and Electricity

What I Used to Think: You have little or no control of your utility bills short of trying to conserve energy and water.

Nobody Told Me: You can manage your utility bills the same way you manage internal operations at your company. Utility companies have complex billing systems you must analyze to help keep down your costs. You can do the research yourself or hire a consultant. I hired a consultant to do the job. Like many utilities consultants, he worked on a commission, splitting the savings with me for a year.

I used to get eight electric bills from eight meters in the 35,000-square-foot building where my business is located. By consolidating those bills, I save $50 to $100 each month. Now that may not seem like a lot of money, but it adds up over the years.

Adjusting when my company uses electricity also has resulted in ongoing savings. Electric companies commonly bill users based on the highest level of their demand. That's why we no longer turn on our lights, computers, and machinery at the same time every morning. Now we turn on half of everything before we open shop and the rest half an hour later. We have significantly reduced the highest level of our demand this way and, hence, our electric bills.

Lesson #125: Trying to lower the cost of your utilities isn't an exercise in futility.

Smart Generosity

What I Used to Think: Give employees the standard 20 percent discount.

Nobody Told Me: It may be worth it to sell your products to employees at cost. I give my employees a 40 percent discount on framing, which is pretty much the same as cost. It encourages them to do a lot of personal framing and gives them a customer's perspective of our products and service. It also makes them feel good about the company.

I don't know how many times I've walked into a shoe store and noticed my salesperson wearing a beat-up pair of old shoes. It doesn't speak well of the company that their employees either can't afford to buy new shoes or don't care enough about the products they're selling to buy them. I always think, "What is this person going to be able to tell me about shoes?"

My employees can offer customers suggestions on mats, frames, glazing, and anything else that has to do with framing based on personal experience. It lends credibility to your company if customers know that your employees use your products or services. That's why it pays to be as generous as you can afford to be with employee discounts.

One problem you may run into is employees passing their discounts along to friends. I avoid this problem by requiring a manager to write up all employee orders and by placing a limit on the amount of merchandise each employee may purchase annually.

I neither want to make nor lose money on employee purchases. Whether or not you want to be generous with employee discounts, you should first know what your costs are and what size of a discount you can afford to give.

Lesson #126: Giving generous employee discounts is as much about being smart as it is about being generous.

The Best Peace of Mind ---- Lockers

What I Used to Think: Employees should be responsible for their own belongings.

Nobody Told Me: Employee lockers help you and your employees avoid a lot of grief. Unfounded suspicions are worse than what the army calls "barracks thieves". I can't tell you how many times employees have come to me accusing other employees of stealing money from their wallets, jackets, or purses.

Employees sometimes do steal from each other. But more often than not, employees are pickpocketed on the way to work, forget they spent $20 on groceries, or don't know family members have taken money from their wallets without asking. It pays to install lockers both to protect your employees from theft, and to prevent false accusations that create an atmosphere of suspicion and distrust.

Lesson #127: Employee lockers are a fringe benefit — to the boss.

Busy Signals

What I Used to Think: Everyone expects a busy signal now and then.

Nobody Told Me: Getting new customers to call you is like winning the lottery. You want to make sure you're there when they call your number. Phone lines are relatively inexpensive. Whatever money you think you're saving by keeping phone lines to a minimum can be lost the minute you lose a phone call.

A few years ago, I wanted some landscaping done. I was having a hard time choosing between two landscapers. I called one guy to tell him that he had the job and got a busy signal. The other landscaper happened to call me twenty minutes later, so I wound up giving the business to him. On many occasions I have called companies listed in the Yellow Pages, got a busy signal, and moved on to the next listing. It's not as if I thought, "I don't want to use this company because they don't have enough phone lines." I just didn't want to wait.

Some companies have too few phone lines because they're trying to save money. Other companies are just too busy to notice that they need additional phone lines. As your company grows, you will more incoming as well as outgoing calls. You need to monitor this increase. The moment someone calls to do business with your company is precious. Guard it with your life.

Lesson #128: If your customers keep getting busy signals, you won't be busy for long.

The Phone Fairy

What I Used to Think: Employees don't abuse telephone privileges.

Nobody Told Me: Many employees imagine that a phone fairy pays for calls to your company's 800 number. When I put in an 800 number a few years ago, I noticed that we were receiving calls on it from all over the country even though I hadn't advertised the number and didn't have customers all over the country. I asked my employees about it and found out they'd given the number to friends and relatives. I'm talking about college-educated employees. Most of them weren't trying to get away with anything. They just had grown up hearing 800 numbers are free. If they had thought about it at all, they may have assumed I pay a flat fee for 800 service. Most, I hope, were unaware their boss pays for each and every call.

Personal long-distance phone calls also present problems. Employees may not realize that a long-distance phone call now and then adds up when you have more than a handful of employees. That's why if you have long-distance service on your phone, you may want to put calling codes on outgoing calls. If you have an 800 number, make sure employees know it's reserved for business calls. It also helps to monitor incoming calls on your 800 line.

Lesson #129: Don't count on the phone fairy to keep your employees in line when it comes to phone privileges.

Don't Be Caught Dead without a Computer System

What I Used to Think: Computer systems are for the big guys.

Nobody Told Me: Computers are vital tools for growing your business. I computerized my business early on, even though my accountant, lawyer, and just about everyone else said I was crazy. The computer system has provided me with greater financial control and has prevented costly mistakes. After I installed my first computer system, I realized how sloppy certain procedures at my company had been.

Computers will help you perform accounting, maintaining customer databases, eliminatie pricing errors, track receivables, monitor inventory, reference old orders; track sales by multiple factors (including geography, sales associate, and product line), and chart average sales, just to name a few important tasks.

Investing in a computer system was costly and painful, but it quickly paid for itself. I confess, I don't know how to use the system. But my company is big enough now that I employ persons who do.

Lesson #130: Great companies have great computer systems.

You're Only as Good as Your Vendors

What I Used to Think: Your vendors wouldn't be in business if they were irresponsible.

Nobody Told Me: There are thriving businesses everywhere that are seriously screwed up. Some of them may be your suppliers. Customer service is one of the main reasons my company is successful, but it's difficult to give great customer service if I get lousy customer service from my suppliers. That's why you have to hold your vendors responsible and be prepared to change vendors if they don't cut it.

I remember a supplier who was supposed to provide my company with a large piece of glass for a specific job. The supplier assured me the glass would be on my dock by noon. There was no sign of the glass at noon, so I called to find out where it was. The supplier told me he was having trouble with his truck. There still was no glass at one o'clock, so I gave him another call. He said the truck had broken down and there would be no delivery that day. I asked if there was anything at all he could do to get the glass to me. He just said, "No."

A responsible company would have put the glass in a cab or arranged for an employee to drive it over. This guy thought a broken-down truck was a good enough reason not to deliver the goods. I changed suppliers and never looked back. I had to go through numerous vendors before I found reliable ones.

The flip side of holding irresponsible vendors accountable is acknowledging those vendors who do a good job for you.

At the end of the year, I send a heartfelt thank-you note or call them to say how much I appreciate their efforts.

Lesson #131: Be as demanding of your vendors as your customers are of you.

Rules Are Meant to Be Written Down

What I Used to Think: Unless you have dozens of rules and regulations, you can do without an employee manual.

Nobody Told Me: Today's legal environment warrants an employee manual, no matter how small your business or how few rules, regulations, policies, and procedures your company has. You also owe it to your employees to provide an easy-to-read reference regarding their employment.

An employee manual can be just a few pages, but if you really want to protect yourself, make it comprehensive. Some issues to address include bereavement leave, lateness to work and vacation pay.

Developing an employee manual forced my managers and me to think through every detail of every company policy and create additional policies. Once you take the step of printing, distributing, and having employees sign off on a manual, you and your managers are obliged to follow it to the letter.

We ask employees to sign a form stating that they have read and understand the employee manual. We keep that form on file. There's little room for confusion or dispute when everything is written down in black and white. My employees know what is expected of them, what they can expect from us, and what they should do if a problem arises. We have few problems with policy violations because employees know what they can and can't do. If we have to fire someone for violating company policy, the person is unlikely to contest it.

You may want to consult with an attorney before embarking on an employee manual. You *must* have an attorney review the copy before you print and distribute it. If you're unsure about what information to include, there are computer software packages and companies that can help you develop an employee manual.

Lesson #132: An employee manual is like a good insurance policy.

Make a Classified Ad Rep's Day

What I Used to Think: Small companies take out small help wanted ads.

Nobody Told Me: A three-line ad may not attract the kind of employees your company needs. You may have to spend extra money for a large ad to find the best prospects for some positions.

When I'm hiring outside sales consultants, I always place a large ad. There's a strong demand for high-caliber outside sales professionals, and the ads in that section reflect this reality. They're bigger and bolder than the ads, for instance, in the retail sales section.

A large ad not only is eye-catching but also lends credibility to your company. Ideally, it attracts more applicants and better-qualified applicants than a small ad. If you're hiring for a low-level position, on the other hand, it probably makes no sense to spend extra money on a large ad.

Lesson #133: The cost of a large help wanted ad is insignificant compared to the benefits of attracting better applicants.

The Upshot

And that's it! What I did right and what I did wrong. I hope you can take this education that I've gained during twenty years in business and put it to great use.

Go get 'em! Remember, opportunity doesn't knock. It lurks. You have to shake the bushes to find it. As for me, I'll be working on Lesson Number 134....

About the Author

Jay Goltz graduated from Northern Illinois University in 1978 with a bachelor of arts degree in accounting. Then, he took what was considered "a different path" and started his own business at a time when most of his peers were taking jobs as accountants or going to graduate school.

In the summer of 1978, Goltz founded Artists' Frame Service in an old factory district in Chicago and has since built it into the largest retail, custom picture framing facility in the nation with over 120 employees.

Goltz has won numerous awards for entrepreneurship, including being inducted into the Entrepreneurship Hall of Fame. He is a frequent public speaker on the subject of entrepreneurship and running a business. In 1997, he started his "Boss School" seminars which he developed for individuals wishing to become better business owners and managers.

Goltz lives in Chicago with his wife Sherri, and his three sons, Mitchell, Aaron, and Jared.

If you are interested in a "Boss School" Seminar or other speaking engagement with Jay Goltz, please write:

Jay Goltz
1915 N. Clybourn Avenue
Chicago, IL 60614
Or call 1-800-444-8387

Index

Addicus Books

Visit the Addicus Books Web Site
http://members.aol.com/addicusbks

The Street-Smart Entrepreneur *133 Tough Lessons I Learned the Hard Way* Jay Goltz, ISBN 1-886039-33-X	*$14.95*
The Healing Touch — Keeping the Doctor/ *Patient Relationship Alive Under Managed Care* David Cram, MD ISBN 1-886039-31-3	*$9.95*
Hello, Methuselah! Living to 100 and Beyond George Webster ISBN 1-886039-259	*$14.95*
The Family Compatibility Test Susan Adams ISBN 1-886039-27-5	*$9.95*
First Impressions — Tips to Enhance Your Image Joni Craighead ISBN 1-886039-26-7	*$14.95*
Straight Talk About Breast Cancer Susan Braddock, MD ISBN 1-886039-21-6	*$9.95*
Prescription Drug Abuse — The Hidden Epidemic Rod Colvin ISBN 1-886030-22-4	*$14.95*
The ABCs of Gold Investing Michael J. Kosares ISBN 1-886039-29-1	*$14.95*
The Flat Tax: Why It Won't Work for America Scott E. Hicko ISBN 1-886039-28-3	*$12.95*

Please send:

_____ copies of _____
                              (Title of book)

at $ _____ each   TOTAL   _____

Nebr. residents add 5% sales tax   _____

Shipping/Handling
  $3.00 for first book.
  $1.00 for each additional book.   _____

TOTAL ENCLOSED   _____

Name_____

Address_____

City _____ State ___ Zip _____

☐ Visa ☐ Master Card ☐ Am. Express

Credit card number _____

Expiration date _____

Order by credit card, personal check or money order.
Send to:

Addicus Books
Mail Order Dept.
P.O. Box 45327
Omaha, NE 68145
Or, order **TOLL FREE: 800-352-2873**